Life & Soul

Celebrate in style with
Emma Forbes

with invitations by
Lucy Clemson of RSVP London

Ivy Press

This book is dedicated to the three people who are the loves of my life and without whom there would be no parties — Graham, Lily & Sam.

First published in the UK in 2011 by

Ivy Press

210 High Street
Lewes
East Sussex BN7 2NS
United Kingdom

www.ivypress.co.uk

ISBN: 978-1-907332-86-9

This book was conceived, designed and produced by
Ivy Press

Creative Director Peter Bridgewater
Publishers Jason Hook & Jenny Manstead
Art Director Wayne Blades
Senior Editor Jayne Ansell
Designer Simon Goggin
Project Manager Dereen Taylor
Photographers Clive & Rob Streeter
Home Economist & Food Stylist Susanna Tee
Design Assistant Edd Lawrence

Printed in China
Colour origination by Ivy Press Reprographics

10 9 8 7 6 5 4 3 2 1

Contents

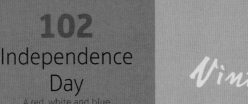

Preface

I have always been someone who loves a party, or more to the point loves throwing a party. From start to finish, I adore the planning, sorting, preparing, cooking and styling. Weirdly I don't like parties for myself – but truly find great pleasure in doing them for others, from children's birthdays to Mother's Day teas and everything in between. I am always thrilled when I have a date in the diary that equals a good excuse for a get-together! I have been hugely lucky to meet fantastic people in my life who share the same passion – so to come together and create this book has been a party in itself!

The team I work with is second to none. Lucy Clemson – a creative force with stylish ideas, energy and the ability to produce seriously original invitations and goody bags that make you go 'Wow'! Lucy's creative involvement in this book really does prove that an invite need never be dull, and that it is quite often the fabulous starting point for creating a fun, innovative and successful party. John Carter – a florist extraordinaire, one of my oldest friends and a man who is truly dedicated to the art of beautiful flowers. John can style flowers that frankly *make* a room, from the simple to the absolutely sensational. Vita Appleby – a totally gorgeous and fabulous cook. She and I love nothing more than a 'cookfest' in the kitchen, spending hours creating new dishes, and, much more importantly and the best bit of all, sampling them! She shares my passion for using only the best ingredients – locally sourced food where possible and always free-range or organic meat and produce. It's truly been a team effort – and what a team!

I think many people are overwhelmed at the thought of throwing a party, as it just seems too big a task. I hope this book will show that you can create all sorts of themes, moods and looks on any budget – easily and with recipes that are big on impact and stress-free to achieve. A book that you can dip in and out of to get ideas for a gathering for any occasion, whether it's to style the room, come up with the menu, find creative inspiration for the invites and goody bags or get the ambiance just right; and, above all, put you in the mood for a party.

So, dip in and let the celebrations begin!

Perfect
Planning

My Recipe for Success

Whether you're entertaining close friends and family, or throwing a big themed bash, the secret to your success depends on the same four key elements…

Choosing your Guests

A winning combination of guests always includes an extrovert to keep the conversation flowing. So be sure to mix your guests so that every group has their own 'life and soul of the party' person. And tempting as it may be, don't always play safe mixing like with like. Sometimes, mixing it up can add a touch of unexpected drama and ensure your party goes with a real swing!

As the host, always make the initial introductions between your guests. Recounting an interesting or special thing about them when introducing them to each other is great for getting the conversation flowing. Then keep an eye on how the groups are working, and be prepared to make some subtle adjustments. Blend two groups together, or if it's a sit-down dinner, encourage your guests to shift two places to the right after each course to ensure that the party spirit is being enjoyed by all and not just some of your guests.

Budgeting

Budgeting may sound boring or even scary, but it's the starting point of all successful party planning. My first three priorities for spending are always invites, food and flowers. Get these right, and with a bit of creativity and a lot of style it's possible to improvise to get the right look for just about everything else. And some of the best ideas really are the cheapest ones… like the bandanna squares we used to make a distinctive tablecloth for Independence Day and the drinks served in baby bottles with straws for Baby Shower.

It's worth saying that you really don't have to follow the styling ideas in this book to the letter. It's much more about dipping in and taking the bits that you like, then heading off and having fun creating your own thriftier or more extravagant version.

Creating your Invite

With the personalized invites Lucy and I created, our aim was always to send something that would excite our guests and make them really want to come to the party, as well as being a fabulous talking point on the night. A great invite captures the mood and prepares for the style of your party.

Do make sure your invite includes all the important information you need your guests to know. If you're planning a sit-down meal, put a set time down so people know and can arrive punctually rather than drift along late. If you are including an RSVP, always remember to put a date by when you'd like to hear back.

Composing your Menu

My absolute top tip for choosing the right menu is to write it down, and then see if you'd choose it at a restaurant!

Make sure your dishes have impact, but that their flavours are not overpowering. Remember, seriously spicy doesn't work for everyone… And find out in advance if any of your guests have special dietary requirements so there are no nasty surprises for you or them on the night.

Quantity can be a tricky one. Too much can look obscene, too little can appear mean. But I'd say it's always better to have leftovers to enjoy the next day than to have to do an emergency dash to the shops because you've run out! Have a plentiful and varied supply of alcoholic and non-alcoholic drinks available too.

The simplest of dishes can look incredible if you put them on a beautiful plate and add the right accessories, like the gorgeous china tea-cups we used for Afternoon Tea. And for Fiesta, wrapping the tacos in napkins tied with raffia was cheap but stunningly effective.

Party Politics

Here's a light-hearted list of 'Party Dos and Don'ts' from the perspective of the perfect host and the perfect guest.

Host Dos

- Do have ground rules that everybody is aware of. Essential at, for example, a fireworks party or a pool party, where there may be safety issues.
- Do make fancy dress achievable. Have a box of spare accessories for those guests who didn't think they wanted to bother but who now want to don a hat or a feather boa.
- Do step back and realize that your guests are enjoying the whole party experience, to which the exquisite finer details have contributed even if they are not being raved over.
- Do employ grace under fire and laugh off any mishaps. The sausages have been cremated? No problem, dip them in some tangy salsa!
- Do have a code word for your family if you're worried you've under-catered on the food. In our house, it's 'FLO', for 'Family Lay Off till the guests are finished'!

And finally… Do plan your party so well in advance that you can relax and get into the party mood on the night!

Host Don'ts

- Don't use the term smart casual. Nobody, and I mean nobody, actually knows what it means.
- Don't over-schedule. Your guests will not appreciate feeling like they are part of some precision-timed military operation.
- Don't get all 'beady' if the finer details of your wonderful party planning don't appear to be appreciated by your guests.
- Don't feel you can't relax and enjoy your own party. If you're stressed your guests will pick up on it and feel guilty about enjoying themselves.

And finally… Don't cry at your own party. Or leave your own party. Ever.

Guest Dos

- Do remember to RSVP, and in plenty of time.
- Do remember to RSVP for 'Save the date' requests too. Your host is testing the water to see who's around, so let them know in plenty of time.
- Do arrive at the right time. If you're early your host won't thank you for it; if you're late they won't thank you for that, either – especially if it's a sit-down meal.
- Do let your host know in advance if you have any special food requirements. And then let it go. There's nothing more mood-dampening than a guest sharing their catalogue of dietary requirements with a table of guests who are about to tuck into a dish of the 'forbidden' food.
- Do be appreciative of the take-home gift, even if it's not 100 per cent your thing. It's the thought that counts!

And finally… Do have fun!

Guest Don'ts

- Don't be a no-show. A no-show, with no advance warning (unless it's a major emergency of course), could well be a strike off a future guest list!
- Don't assume it's open season and you can take anything from one extra person to a troupe of extra people along with you, unless you've politely asked in advance.
- Don't turn up empty-handed. Every host will appreciate a thoughtful gesture, whether it's home-made truffles, or a pretty bunch of flowers from the garden.
- Don't turn up ill or with ill children.
- Don't diet at someone else's party. Diet on your own time, not theirs.

And finally… Don't be afraid to muck in with the clearing up at the end. Your host will love you for it!

Party People

I would love to say I organize fabulous parties at the drop of a hat. But actually, it just wouldn't be possible without a little help from my friends…

Lucy Clemson

I was lucky enough to find the amazingly creative and lovely Lucy when I was googling for bespoke invites for my son Sam's eleventh birthday party. As well as sharing my passion for a good party, Lucy has the fantastic ability to come up with a special and unique invite for every occasion. For Sam's birthday, she pulled out all the stops for something deceptively simple, with a total 'wow' factor, coming up with an invite that I loved but am just not creative enough to dream up myself! And from there what's developed is a beautiful, fun friendship, and a succession of gorgeous and completely original invites for every party I've thrown since. And I'm happy to confirm that a creative and personal invite really does ensure your guest is excited to accept and can't wait to come to the party!

www.rsvplondon.com

John Carter

My first memory of the adorable John goes back over twenty years, when he worked for Sir Terence Conran at the Conran Shop in London. Whenever I drove past, I would be drawn to John's show-stopping floral displays and would stop to chat and buy armfuls of his amazing flowers. From this, a very special friendship 'blossomed', and John is now one of my oldest, dearest friends. John's flair and passion have really helped me appreciate the importance of fresh flowers and how choosing the right ones can absolutely make a party table. And it's nothing to do with cost… he's shown me how single stems from the garden can sometimes be the perfect finishing touch. I love John and I love flowers, and we often say that in another life I would have made him a rather good assistant!

www.johncarterflowers.com

Vita Appleby

My path first crossed with the beautiful Vita's when she gave cookery lessons to my daughter. A friendship developed between the two of us, based around our shared love of food… 'Yum' is pretty much all you can hear when we are in the kitchen together! Vita and I share a belief that cooking should be fun and never stressful. Our idea of a day well-spent is having a massive cook-a-thon, chatting, laughing and filling the freezer with delicious, tasty food, then kicking back with a glass of something nicely chilled. We've spent many a happy hour developing spicy dips and zesty lemon squares, and we always love creating anything with chocolate in it! So dedicated to the cause are we that during the making of this book, we ate our way to what I hope you'll agree is the perfect savoury muffin!

My Style Directory

Here are my top sources for finding useful party essentials and those gorgeous extras to make your party something truly special.

www.cakecraftshop.co.uk – interesting packaging for home-baked goodies

www.cathkidston.co.uk – great supplier for pretty picnicware, plates, glasses and tablecloths

www.cupcakewrappers.co.uk – gorgeous cupcake wrappers and a whole lot more

www.designersguild.com – wonderful coloured china, tableware and linens

www.everythingstopsfortea.com – a glorious one-stop shop for everything you could need for the perfect vintage tea party

www.forbesstyle.com – my own website full of fabulous tips, ideas and stylish things to buy and try!

www.giftbagshop.co.uk – great for bags to fill with goodies, including organza gift bags

www.honeytreepublishing.com – wonderful for bespoke labels that can be attached to gifts

www.lakeland.co.uk – a wide range of baking and cooking accessories

www.maccorns.co.uk – my go-to for ordering popcorn in bulk

www.millymollymandy.net – take a look for really pretty and unusual muffin wraps and cases

www.mymms.com – add personalized messages to your M&Ms for a fun talking point at your party

www.rsvplondon.com – stunning original invitations

www.starbags.info – great for bespoke party bags if you don't have the time to prepare them yourself!

www.vvrouleaux.com – the best ribbons ever

www.williams-sonoma.com – offers a fabulous range of useful and stylish cooking tools and tablewear

www.zarahome.com – less expensive table accessories

Relaxed

♥ beach party ♥

*Oh, I really do like to be beside the seaside...
it's the perfect setting for a gloriously
old-fashioned picnic party!*

Flag it
*If you can hand deliver your invite,
go for a cute little bucket filled with
sand and topped with a flag containing
all the party details.*

My dream beach party is an old-fashioned picnic. Inspired by those classic Enid Blyton picture books, it's all about red and white gingham checks, fishing nets and home-made lemonade. The aim is to create something fun and relaxed, but still stylish and special. Let your fabulous surroundings inspire your decor. Younger members of the party will love going off on a treasure hunt to find pretty seashells, cute starfish, crispy seaweed and weathered driftwood that you can use to customize your setting. Bring your picnic in a traditional hamper or those lovely, old-fashioned wicker baskets. I like to keep it simple, with tasty, wholesome dishes that guests can enjoy eating with their fingers from a napkin. Have fun with a seaside-inspired menu – stuffed pasta shells and jellies served in miniature buckets with a starfruit on the side. Be prepared to work with the weather – take kites for a windy day, sun shades for a scorching hot one and blankets and sweaters if it's chilly. Get all the ingredients right and a simple picnic could turn into a gloriously long day of fun and freedom on the beach. Just remember to watch out for the tide!

Splashes of colour
Starting with a red-and-white checked picnic blanket, it's easy to add colour and interest with a few striking blue, green, red and yellow accessories.

Mix & match *(below & right)*
Bring along a few beach-inspired accessories, and then scour the beach for interesting extras, like driftwood, seashells and starfish.

Catch of the day
Home-made cordial in old-fashioned stoppered bottles captures the sweetness and innocence of times gone by.

Bucket & spade
In all the fun of planning the perfect picnic, decor and accessories, don't forget to pack good old buckets, spades and fishing nets!

Has anyone got…?
Be prepared, with a bucket full of sunscreen, plasters, insect spray and anything else your guests may need to make their day on the beach more comfortable.

Retro details
Encourage your guests to leave the high-tech world behind for a few hours with fabulously retro pieces that recreate a slower, more relaxed bygone era.

Lashings of lemonade
Why not serve refreshing home-made lemonade in cute jam jars with straws?

Take-home treat *(left)*
Add personalized labels to stripy sticks of rocks for a fun take-home gift for your guests. 'Kiss me quick!' is always a winner.

Wish you were here *(right)*
These cheeky seaside postcard invites perfectly capture the jolly, retro feel of the picnic and make a great alternative if the bucket of sand invite isn't practical.

Come to our BEACH PICNIC!
Sunday 5 June at 1pm
on St Ives Beach

"Oh Donald, do bury me in the sand!"

Fill tealight holders with shells and pebbles for gorgeously simple decorations.

Relaxed

picnic salad baskets

assemble these delicious little baskets at home, then dress the salad at the picnic

TO MAKE THE SALAD BASKETS

- Preheat the oven to 200°C/400°F/Gas 6. Cut the crusts off the bread slices. Brush each slice of bread with 1 teaspoon of oil (this should be enough for both sides). Line a 12-hole muffin tin with the slices of bread, using your fingers to push them carefully into the tin. These should look rather untidy and hang over the edge of the muffin hole.

- Bake in the oven for 10 minutes, until golden and crispy around the edges. Allow to cool slightly in the tin then transfer to a wire rack. Allow the baskets to cool completely before stuffing with salad or the heat will make the salad limp.

- To make the dressing, put the lemon juice into a small bowl. Add the salt and mix with a spoon until dissolved. Add the oil and season to taste with pepper. Mix well until the olive oil and lemon juice have amalgamated, then pour into an empty jam jar or 6 miniature jam jars.

- To prepare the salad, cut the tomatoes into quarters. Peel, deseed and finely dice the cucumber.

- When the bread baskets are cold, stuff with the tops of the Cos lettuce, using 2–3 leaves per basket. Chop the rest of the leaf and put in the bottom of the basket. Add a few quartered tomatoes and lastly a sprinkling of the diced cucumber. Wrap these up, undressed, to take to your picnic.

- At the picnic, make sure the lid is on tightly and vigorously shake the dressing. Pour over your salad-filled bread baskets and eat immediately!

SERVES	PREP/COOKING
6	25 mins/10 mins

INGREDIENTS
12 thin slices brown or white bread
4 tbsp olive oil

FOR THE SALAD
200g/7oz cherry tomatoes
½ cucumber
2 Cos lettuces

FOR THE DRESSING
2 tbsp lemon juice (about 1 lemon)
½ tsp salt
4 tbsp extra virgin olive oil
freshly ground black pepper

bucket of sand jelly

the starfruit starfish are such a cute addition to these

TO MAKE THE JELLY

- ♥ Make up 1 packet of jelly according to the instructions on the packet. Pour into the buckets and leave in the refrigerator for 2 hours, until set.
- ♥ Thinly slice the starfruit widthways to make star shapes. Place 1 slice of starfruit on top of the set jelly in each bucket.
- ♥ Make up the second packet of jelly. Leave to cool for 20 minutes and then pour on top of the set jelly, which will give the illusion that the star is suspended in the middle. Leave the jelly to set for a further 2 hours.
- ♥ When set, decorate each bucket of jelly with a slice of starfruit.

MAKES	PREP
6	10 mins
	(plus cooling and setting time)

INGREDIENTS

2 x 135g packets lemon-
    flavoured jelly
3 starfruit

Relaxed

seaside picnic pasta

decorate with these adorable seashell cocktail sticks

TO MAKE THE PASTA

- ♥ Cook the pasta according to the instructions on the packet. Drain, toss in the olive oil to prevent it from sticking together, and leave to cool completely.
- ♥ Put the lemon juice, yogurt and mayonnaise in a large bowl and mix together into a smooth sauce. Add the drained sweetcorn and tuna and mix together. Season to taste with pepper.
- ♥ Generously stuff each pasta shell with the tuna mixture. Serve piled high on a bed of samphire, if using.

SERVES
6

PREP & COOKING
30 mins

INGREDIENTS

250g/9oz large pasta shells

1 tbsp olive oil

1 tsp lemon juice

2 tbsp Greek yogurt

2 tbsp mayonnaise

326g canned sweetcorn, drained

2 x 200g cans tuna in olive oil, drained

freshly ground black pepper

100g/3½oz samphire, to serve (optional)

apple turnovers
serve on a nest of red-and-white checked napkins

TO MAKE THE APPLE TURNOVERS

- ♥ Preheat the oven to 200°C/400°F/Gas 6. Line a baking tray with baking paper.
- ♥ Peel, core and finely chop the apples. Put the butter in a saucepan and melt over a low heat. Add the apples and lemon juice and simmer for 2–3 minutes until soft. Stir occasionally to make sure they are not catching on the bottom of the pan.
- ♥ Remove the pan from the heat and stir in the sugar, reserving 1 tablespoon for later.
- ♥ Cut the pastry into 6 squares, each measuring about 10x10cm/ 4x4in. Carefully place the squares on the prepared baking tray.
- ♥ Put the cooked apples into the centre of the pastry. Brush a little water onto 2 adjoining edges of the pastry squares. Lift over a corner to meet the opposite corner and seal the edges by pushing down with your fingertips. Repeat with the remaining squares.
- ♥ Make a small hole in the top of the pastry to allow the steam to escape and prevent the seams bursting open. Beat the egg yolk and milk together and brush over the tops of the turnovers. Sprinkle over the remaining sugar.
- ♥ Bake in the oven for 15–20 minutes, until golden brown.

MAKES
6

PREP/COOKING
30 mins/15–20 mins

INGREDIENTS
3 dessert apples, such as Royal Gala, Braeburn or Cox's
10g/¼oz unsalted butter
1 tsp lemon juice
50g/1¾oz golden caster sugar
375g/13oz ready-rolled puff pastry
1 egg yolk
1 tbsp milk

Beach Party

♥ brunch ♥

*What's not to love about a brunch party?
It's an opportunity to spend a few lazy hours
grazing on good food and enjoying great company.*

Relaxation in progress

*A great invite manages to say it all
in a simple but original way. And this
'Do not disturb' door hanger does just
that, leaving your guests in no doubt
that they are being invited to relax
and hang out.*

DO NOT DISTURB
Relaxation
IN PROGRESS
Join us for an afternoon of
brunch and laid-back fun
on Sunday 28th February from
11am – 4pm
4 Park Terrace, London W4

On a lazy Sunday morning (often following a not-so-lazy Saturday night!), I love throwing a brunch party. It's a very laid-back, no beginning and no end kind of thing, where friends are welcome to just drop by. Create the right chilled-out atmosphere, and even the most 'active' types can be seduced, usually with the aroma of fresh coffee and the draw of bagging the last corner of the jigsaw! I always think a really strong, simple colour scheme works well for this time of day, with crisp white linen and tablewear, and wicker baskets in rich shades of chocolate and coffee. Then add vibrant bursts of sunshine with golden sunflowers and piles of oranges. Go for appetizing and inviting food that will encourage your guests to pick and graze, while they chat and read the papers. A mix of sweet and savoury works really well, with fritatta and soggy honey cake and loads of freshly squeezed orange juice. And if you or one of your guests fancies a slot as a short order chef, you can also offer pancakes and eggs. Put on a bit of Louis Armstrong in the background, then kick back and savour the mood.

Thank you for coming
Send your guests off with a gorgeous bunch of in-season flowers wrapped in a newspaper and crossword, so they can continue the relaxing at home.

Everybody's welcome
The laid-back mood of a brunch party means that it crosses the ages, and even suits beloved family pets like Scooby here!

Big on coffee
French-style oversized cups and saucers hold really generous amounts of coffee, meaning less getting up for a refill!

Sunny side up
Go for bright and cheerful flowers – bunches of large sunflowers are perfect – to bring warmth and sunshine to the party.

Brunch is served
I think heavy, crisp white napkins sum up the 'late breakfast at a boutique hotel' vibe perfectly.

Hanging around (left)
Why not display your fabulous invite as a gentle reminder that it really is all about kicking back and hanging out…

Phone-free zone (below)
A basket by the front door means your guests can free themselves of their mobile phones as they come in and really 'switch off'.

Game on
Have a stockpile of board games for your guests, should they feel the need to dabble in something a bit more active!

DO NOT DISTURB

Relaxation IN PROGRESS

Join us for an afternoon of brunch and laid-back fun on Sunday 28th February from

11am – 4pm

4 Park Terrace, London W4

'Real' coffee
Treat your guests to a cup of 'real' coffee, either from a cafetière or an espresso machine. They'll love it, and the coffee bean aroma will be divine!

Freshly squeezed
There's nothing quite as refreshing as a glass of freshly squeezed orange juice, particularly for those guests who've partied too hard the night before!

I love the whole
'lazy start to the day'
feel that the perfect
brunch creates.

Relaxed

cheesy sun-dried tomato & oregano muffins
delicious served warm

TO MAKE THE MUFFINS

- Preheat the oven to 170°C/325°F/Gas 3. Line a 12-hole muffin tin with paper cases. Melt the butter and set aside. Grate the cheese.
- Spread the tomatoes on a sheet of kitchen paper, put 2–3 more sheets on top and press down to blot up any excess oil. Remove the paper and chop the tomatoes into small pieces.
- In a large bowl, mix together the flour, baking powder, bicarbonate of soda, sugar, salt, oregano and grated cheese. Add the chopped tomatoes and stir again until everything is coated with flour.
- Whisk the milk and yogurt together, and then whisk in the eggs, one at a time.
- Make a well in the centre of the flour. Pour in the egg mixture and then add the melted butter. Gently stir with a wooden spoon until only just combined (the trick for a light, fluffy muffin is not to stir the mixture too vigorously and it's very important to stop stirring when the mixture only just comes together). Spoon the mixture equally into the paper cases.
- Bake in the oven for 20 minutes, until lightly golden on top. Leave in the tin for 2–3 minutes before transferring to a wire rack and leaving to cool (this will prevent the bottoms of the muffins from going soggy).

MAKES
12

PREP/COOKING
25 mins/20 mins

INGREDIENTS
80g/3oz unsalted butter

150g/5½oz mature Cheddar cheese

280g jar sun-dried tomatoes in oil, drained

250g/9oz plain white flour

2 tsp baking powder

½ tsp bicarbonate of soda

2 tsp caster sugar

¼ tsp salt

1 tbsp dried oregano

100ml/3½fl oz milk

100g/3½oz Greek yogurt

2 medium eggs

pancetta & potato frittata

not only easy to make, but looks and tastes divine

TO MAKE THE FRITTATA

- ♥ Preheat the grill to high.
- ♥ Cut the pancetta into cubes. Dice the potatoes and finely chop the onions.
- ♥ Using a large, non-stick frying pan, fry the pancetta over a medium heat for 2–3 minutes. Add the diced potatoes and fry for about 5 minutes, stirring occasionally, until the potatoes begin to soften and get slightly crispy edges but are not burnt.
- ♥ When the potatoes are soft enough to push a sharp knife through, add the finely chopped onions, thyme and salt and pepper to taste. Stir well together, making sure the heat is not so high that it burns the bottom of the pan. Fry for a further 1 minute until the onions soften.
- ♥ Beat the eggs together and season well with salt and pepper. Pour the eggs into the pan to cover the potatoes and pancetta. (Do not mix or you will end up with scrambled egg!) Turn the heat up and cook the eggs for 3 minutes, until set.
- ♥ Place the pan under the grill and cook for 5 minutes until the top is golden. (If your grill is very hot, keep a watchful eye on the frittata as the top will burn easily.)
- ♥ Serve sprinkled with chopped tomatoes and parsley.

SERVES	PREP & COOKING
12	30 mins

INGREDIENTS

140g/5oz pancetta

3 handfuls new potatoes
   (about 15 potatoes)

2 white or red onions

1 tbsp fresh or dried thyme

8 medium eggs

salt and freshly ground
   black pepper

TO GARNISH

chopped tomatoes

chopped fresh flat-leaf parsley

Relaxed

retox cocktail
for those who like a kick to their brunch

TO MAKE THE COCKTAIL

- ❤ Put the ice into a tall glass. Pour in the vodka and then the tomato juice. Add the lemon juice, Tabasco, if using, adding more or less according to taste, and the Worcestershire sauce. Stir together and season to taste with salt and pepper.
- ❤ Serve with celery sticks and long sticks of cucumber.

SERVES	PREP
1	3 mins

INGREDIENTS

handful of ice cubes
2 shots vodka, preferably chilled
300ml/½ pint tomato juice
juice of ½ lemon
2 dashes Tabasco sauce (optional)
5 dashes Worcestershire sauce
salt and freshly ground
    black pepper
celery sticks, to serve (optional)
cucumber sticks, to serve (optional)

detox smoothie
the healthy, refreshing option

TO MAKE THE SMOOTHIE

- ❤ Break the bananas into chunks and put in a blender. Add all the remaining ingredients and blitz for 2–3 minutes, until it is a smooth consistency.
- ❤ Serve in tumblers with a wedge of peach on the side and a few sprigs of mint.

SERVES	PREP
6	4 mins

INGREDIENTS

4 bananas
300g/10½oz blueberries
600ml/1 pint peach juice or white
    grape and peach juice
4 tbsp chopped fresh mint
juice of 2 limes
2 tbsp Greek yogurt
1 peach, to serve (optional)
mint sprigs, to garnish (optional)

soggy honey cake

blueberries and honey go together just beautifully

TO MAKE THE CAKE

- ♥ Preheat the oven to 180°C/350°F/Gas 4. Grease a 20cm/8in round or square cake tin. Sift the flour and baking powder together into a bowl.
- ♥ In an electric mixer, or using a large mixing bowl and an electric hand-held mixer, beat the butter and sugar together until light and fluffy, and then beat in the eggs.
- ♥ Add the yogurt and 4 tablespoons of the honey and mix well together. Add the sifted flour and almonds and stir well together. Spoon the mixture into the prepared tin.
- ♥ Bake in the oven for 25 minutes, until risen and golden, and a knife inserted in the centre comes out clean. If, after 20 minutes, the cake is browning too quickly, cover with a sheet of foil. Remove from the oven and make holes with a fork all over the top. Spread over the remaining 2 tbsp of honey and the lemon juice. Re-cover, if necessary, and then return to the oven and bake for a further 5 minutes.
- ♥ To serve, either leave to cool and cut into squares, or serve warm with Greek yogurt mixed with manuka honey and berries. Before serving, drizzle with extra honey and dust with sifted icing sugar to decorate.

SERVES
6–8

PREP/COOKING
20 mins/30 mins

INGREDIENTS

175g/6oz plain white flour

2 tsp baking powder

100g/3½oz butter

40g/1½oz caster sugar

2 medium eggs

2 heaped tbsp Greek yogurt

6 tbsp clear honey, plus extra
   for drizzling

55g/2oz ground almonds

juice of 1 lemon

Greek yogurt, manuka honey
   and berries, if serving warm

icing sugar, for dusting

♥ no-hassle dinner ♥

In my experience, some of the most memorable parties are the spontaneous ones!

Instant invite
To save time, why not text the invite to your guests? Now that really is no-hassle!

I promise you, it really is possible to entertain at home without it being scary or overwhelming! And without numerous trips to the fishmonger, greengrocer or deli, too. A no-hassle party works best with those guests you can comfortably invite at the last minute, rather than weeks in advance. For my 40th birthday, I was determined not to have a big celebration. On the day, my husband Graham gave me a wonderful video of special family moments that I really wanted to share. So we invited close family and friends round for a viewing, followed by a quickly rustled-up shepherd's pie round the kitchen table. With a few stylish touches, such as single flowers in pretty glass vases and masses of candles, it was spontaneous, simple and relaxed, and truly one of the best evenings we've ever had! The key to no-hassle success is the menu – using store-cupboard favourites and what's in your fridge to create maximum impact for minimum effort and hassle. Go on, give it a go!

Easy does it
Relaxed and simple… it's all about the tasty, wholesome food and the pretty place settings.

Pretty as a flower
*Go for a light, airy feel,
with clusters of delicate
glass vases containing
beautiful flowers.*

Cheap but very cheerful
Knives and forks wrapped in pretty, mismatched napkins look lovely. And it's a great way of using odd leftover napkins too!

Scent-sational *(left)*
Old perfume bottles make original vases that look fabulous when grouped together.

All wrapped up *(right)*
Why not cook extra dessert for your guests to take home? Then all you need to make charming parcels is rickrack ribbon and napkins.

Clusters of candles
Clusters of flickering scented candles look beautiful, smell divine and help create an intimate, relaxed atmosphere.

Take-away gift
If you would like to give your guests a more substantial take-home gift, package the dessert macaroons in these sweet take-away boxes and add a personal tag.

Warming, tasty food, good company and a
relaxed host. Now that's a recipe for a party!

macaroni cheese with caramelized leeks

comfort food at its best

TO MAKE THE MACARONI CHEESE

- ♥ Thinly slice the leeks. Over a low heat, melt the butter in a large saucepan, add the leeks and thyme and cook for about 5 minutes, stirring occasionally, until soft and slightly browned.
- ♥ Cook the pasta in a large saucepan of boiling salted water, according to the instructions on the packet.
- ♥ Meanwhile, make the cheese sauce. Grate the cheese. Melt the butter in a saucepan over a low heat. When melted, add the flour and stir continuously for about 1 minute, until it turns slightly lighter in colour. The most important thing is not to let it darken and burn!
- ♥ Add 100ml/3½fl oz of the milk and whisk in quickly until it amalgamates with the butter and flour mixture. Add 200ml/7fl oz of the milk and continue to stir. When the sauce thickens, add another 200ml/7fl oz of the milk and repeat until all the milk has been incorporated. The sauce will take slightly longer to thicken each time you add a quantity of milk so continue stirring for a further 5 minutes after all the milk has been added. Season to taste with salt and pepper.
- ♥ Remove the pan from the heat and stir in the mustard, the grated cheese and the cooked leeks.
- ♥ Preheat the grill to high. Drain the cooked pasta and tip it into the pan of cheese sauce. (If your pan is not large enough, mix the pasta and sauce together in a large bowl.) Coat the pasta in the glorious cheesy leek sauce before transferring to an ovenproof dish.
- ♥ Mix the breadcrumbs and Parmesan together and sprinkle over the top of the macaroni cheese. Cook under the grill for 3–5 minutes, until golden.

SERVES	PREP & COOKING
4–6	30 mins

INGREDIENTS

3 leeks

25g/1oz butter

2 tsp dried thyme

400g/14oz macaroni

1 tbsp fresh breadcrumbs

1 tbsp freshly grated
   Parmesan cheese

FOR THE CHEESE SAUCE

200g/7oz mature Cheddar cheese

50g/1¾oz butter

3 tbsp plain white flour

700ml/1¼pints semi-skimmed
   or whole milk

2 tsp Dijon mustard

salt and freshly ground
   black pepper

garlic & herb bread
simple, rustic and tastes delicious

TO MAKE THE BREAD

- ♥ Preheat the oven to 200°C/400°F/Gas 6.
- ♥ Crush or very finely chop the garlic and finely chop the herbs. Put the butter, garlic and herbs in a bowl and mash together. Season to taste with salt and pepper.
- ♥ Cut large, diagonal wedges into the bread. Remove the wedges and discard so that you will be left with a loaf of bread that looks like it has a spiky top.
- ♥ Generously spread the garlic butter into the spaces of the bread. Wrap in foil but keep the top open.
- ♥ Bake in the oven for 10 minutes. Serve in the foil parcel.

SERVES
6

PREP/COOKING
15mins/10mins

INGREDIENTS
3 garlic cloves

1–2 handfuls of fresh herbs, such as flat- or curly-leaf parsley and basil

150g/5½oz unsalted butter, at room temperature

1 unsliced farmhouse loaf, ciabatta or baguette

salt and freshly ground black pepper

american chopped salad

it's the fabulous colours that make this simple salad so special

TO MAKE THE SALAD

- Prepare all the salad ingredients and place in a bowl. Cut the carrot into 1cm/½in cubes. Remove the core and seeds from the red pepper and cut the flesh into 1cm/½in cubes. Peel and cut the cucumber into 1cm/½in cubes. Cut the tomatoes and radishes into eighths. Thinly slice and then roughly chop the lettuces. Crumble or cut the cheese into cubes. Finely chop the ham and parsley. Very finely chop the gherkin, and the onion, if using.
- If you have a clean, empty jam jar, it is perfect for making the salad dressing. Alternatively, use a small bowl. Squeeze the lemon juice into your jar or bowl, removing any pips. Add the salt and mix with a spoon until dissolved. Add honey and mix until dissolved. Add the oil and season to taste with pepper. Screw the lid tightly on the jar and shake vigorously, or mix well with a spoon in the bowl.
- Just before serving, shake or stir the dressing, pour over the salad and toss together.

SERVES	PREP
6	25 mins

INGREDIENTS

1 carrot

1 red pepper

½ cucumber

15 cherry tomatoes

8 radishes

4 Little Gem lettuces

200g/7oz feta, mozzarella or
    goats' cheese

120g/4¼oz ham slices

2 handfuls fresh flat-leaf parsley

1 large gherkin

½ red onion (optional)

FOR THE DRESSING

2 tbsp lemon juice (about
    1 lemon)

½ tsp salt

2 tsp clear honey

4 tbsp extra virgin olive oil

freshly ground black pepper

fruit salad

it's the grated coconut that really makes this

TO MAKE THE FRUIT SALAD

- ♥ Prepare the fruit and put it in a large serving bowl. Cut the grapes in half and the strawberries into quarters. Slice the bananas no thicker than 1cm/½in. Peel and core the apples and cut into 1cm/½in cubes. If using, peel and cut the Sharon fruit into 1cm/½in cubes.
- ♥ Grate the coconut. Add to the fruit with the honey and gently mix together. Store in the refrigerator until ready to serve.

SERVES	PREP
6	25 mins

INGREDIENTS

150g/5½oz black grapes

250g/9oz strawberries

2 bananas

2 dessert apples, such as
   Royal Gala

2 Sharon fruit (optional)

30g/1oz fresh coconut

1 tbsp clear honey

coconut macaroons
edible food glitter adds some sparkle

TO MAKE THE MACAROONS

- Preheat the oven to 200°C/400°F/Gas 6. Line a baking sheet with rice paper or baking paper.
- In a bowl, whisk the egg and the egg whites together until pale in colour and creamy. Add the sugar, coconut and vanilla extract and mix well together.
- With your hands, form the coconut mixture into small rounds, about the size of a dessertspoon, patting it together. Place on the prepared baking sheet.
- Bake in the oven for 15–20 minutes, until golden brown on the outside but sticky and gooey in the middle. Leave to cool.
- Serve sprinkled with edible food glitter.

MAKES	PREP/COOKING
4–6	20 mins/15–20 mins

INGREDIENTS

1 whole medium egg and
  2 egg whites
100g/3½oz caster sugar
200g/7oz desiccated coconut
½ tsp vanilla extract
edible gold glitter, to decorate

Special
Occasion

♥ christmas celebration ♥

With a few new ideas alongside favourite family traditions you can create a fabulously festive feel that will wow your guests.

Under the mistletoe
Harking back to the lovely Christmas tradition where a man and a woman who meet under it are obliged to kiss, a prettily tied sprig of mistletoe makes the perfect festive invite. If you're posting your invites, carefully roll them into small gold tubes to protect the fresh mistletoe during its journey.

You are invited to our
CHRISTMAS PARTY!
Join the cosy festive fun from 8pm onwards on 18th December
35 Shawfield Street, London SW3 4BD

Everyone has their own special way of celebrating Christmas. For some it's about indulging in childhood traditions, and for others it's a time to relax with family and friends before the new year begins. Me? I love every bit of it, from decorating the tree to shedding a tear at the children's carol concert. My attitude is very much, 'It only comes once a year, so let's make it special and enjoy it!' As a host, it's about making your guests feel welcome. So make sure your home is cosy, warm and inviting, full of rich colours, wonderful food and the delicious aromas of spicy pine and warm cinnamon. Go the whole nine yards, hanging a gloriously festive wreath on your front door, playing Christmas carols and hanging large bunches of mistletoe tied with thick red ribbon over doorways. Then indulge in every fun decoration fantasy that you have, whether it's hanging home-made stockings by the fire or, a particular Christmas soft spot of mine, displaying clusters of snow globes. Go on… have some festive fun!

Christmas calm
I love that quiet moment when everything's come together and you're just waiting for your guests to arrive…

Festive bits
Look out for interesting and versatile decorations, like this reindeer that makes a lovely holder for chocolate coins!

All wrapped up
Brown wrapping paper is inexpensive, and looks fantastic with pretty ribbon and a personalized label.

Christmas tree magic
A real tree doesn't just make a great focal point, but also fills the room with that gorgeous fresh pine aroma that just says 'Christmas'.

A cracker of a napkin
Instead of crackers, make your guests a festive treat made up of mistletoe, chocolate coins and a small gift wrapped in a napkin. Why not include your own joke or forfeit inside?

Floral success
Dark red velvet roses and bright berries – the perfect festive floral combination.

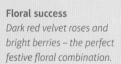

Tom

Relax... *(above)*
A crackling log fire really invites your guests to sit, chat and relax.

A place to be *(left)*
Personalized place settings make your guests feel special, and show you've gone that extra mile to welcome them.

Berry nice
Masses of deep green pine and holly and beautiful red berries, with an added bit of sparkle, make such an impact in the centre of the table.

Christmas colours
I love a traditional Christmas palette – deep red, green and gold. Rich and opulent, it looks fabulous in an over-the-top kind of way!

beef pies

treat your guests to indulgent individual pies

TO MAKE THE PIES

- Cut the meat into bite-sized chunks. Dry with kitchen paper and then dust with the flour. Thinly slice the onions and cut the mushrooms into quarters.
- Heat 1 tablespoon of the oil in a large flameproof casserole dish. Add the meat and fry, in batches if necessary, until browned on all sides. (Don't overcrowd the pan because the meat will then steam and you won't achieve the lovely brown crust that you want.) Remove the meat from the pan.
- Add the onions and remaining 1 tablespoon of oil to the pan and cook over a low heat for about 5 minutes, until softened. Return the meat to the pan, add the stock, tomato purée, sugar, nutmeg and salt and season to taste with pepper. Bring to the boil, stir and then cover with the lid.
- Reduce the heat to low and simmer very gently for 1 hour, until the meat is tender. Remove the pan from the heat, add the mushrooms and the peas, if using, and leave to cool.
- To serve, preheat the oven to 200°C/400°F/Gas 6. Put 6 200ml/ 7 fl oz pie dishes on a baking tray.
- Fill each pie dish two-thirds full with the meat filling. Put the egg yolk and milk in a cup and mix together.
- Roll out the pastry on a lightly floured surface to 5mm/¼in thickness. Cut off 2cm/¾in strips from around the edge of the pastry and put the strips around the edge of the pie dishes. Cut the rolled-out pastry into 6 pieces, slightly larger than the pie dishes. Brush the strips of pastry with the egg wash and put the pieces of pastry on top of the pies. Trim the edges and then seal with your thumb. Brush the egg wash on top of the pies. Any leftover pastry can be cut into leaves and used to decorate the pies, securing them in place with a little egg wash. Make a small hole in the centre to allow steam to escape during cooking.
- Bake in the oven for 15–20 minutes, until the pies are golden brown. Serve with roasted vegetables and a green bean salad.

MAKES	PREP/COOKING
6	45 mins/
	1 hr 15–20mins

INGREDIENTS

500g/1lb 2oz chuck or stewing
   steak
1 tbsp plain white flour,
   plus extra for rolling
2 red onions
50g/1¾oz button mushrooms
2 tbsp olive oil
400ml/14fl oz beef stock
3 tbsp tomato purée
1 tsp soft brown sugar
½ tsp grated nutmeg
1 tsp salt
50g/1¾oz frozen petit pois peas
   (optional)
800g/1lb 12oz puff pastry
1 egg yolk
1 tbsp milk
salt and freshly ground
   black pepper

roasted vegetables
a delicious accompaniment to the pies

TO MAKE THE VEGETABLES

- Preheat the oven to 180°C/350°F/Gas 4.
- Cut the parsnips lengthways into wedges. Peel and cut the butternut squash into wedges. Cut the courgettes into 2cm/¾in chunks. Core and deseed the red pepper and cut into large chunks.
- Put the parsnips and potatoes in a large saucepan of water. Bring to the boil then reduce the heat and simmer for 5 minutes. Drain well.
- Put the parsnips, potatoes and prepared vegetables into a large roasting tin and add the leeks. Finally add the tomatoes so that they cover the vegetables.
- Drizzle over the olive oil, sprinkle over the rosemary and season well with salt and pepper.
- Roast in the oven for 45 minutes–1 hour, until the edges of the parsnips are slightly crisp and the potatoes are soft.

SERVES	PREP/COOKING
6	25 mins/45–60 mins

INGREDIENTS

2 large parsnips

1 butternut squash

2 courgettes

1 red pepper

300g/10½oz new potatoes

10–15 baby leeks

150g/5½oz cherry vine tomatoes

4 tbsp olive oil

1 tbsp finely chopped fresh
　rosemary

salt and freshly ground
　black pepper

Special Occasion

sticky banana gingerbread

the perfect alternative to traditional Christmas treats

TO MAKE THE GINGERBREAD

- Preheat the oven to 180°C/350°F/Gas 4. Line a shallow 20cm/ 8in square brownie tin with baking paper.
- In a large bowl, cream the butter and sugar together until light and fluffy. Add the eggs, one at a time, and beat together.
- In another bowl, sift the flour, baking powder and ground ginger together. Gradually add to the butter mixture in spoonfuls, beating the mixture well until it becomes lighter and fluffier. Stir in the grated ginger and add the milk to form a smooth dropping consistency.
- Thinly slice the bananas and use to line the bottom of the prepared cake tin. Drizzle over about 2 tablespoons of the golden syrup to just cover the bananas. Add the cake mixture to cover the bananas, taking care not to dislodge any of the banana slices.
- Bake in the oven for 25–35 minutes, until risen and golden brown. A knife inserted in the centre should come out clean.
- Remove from the oven and leave to cool slightly before turning the cake out by inverting the baking tin onto a large plate. Gently peel off the baking paper, being careful that the bananas stay in place. While still warm, drizzle more golden syrup over the top so that it is really sticky.
- To serve, cut into squares and serve warm with vanilla ice cream or cold, piled onto a serving plate.

SERVES
8

PREP/COOKING
25 mins/25–30 mins

INGREDIENTS

200g/7oz unsalted butter, at room temperature

200g/7oz light brown muscovado sugar

3 large eggs

275g/9 ½oz plain white flour

3 tsp baking powder

2 tsp ground ginger

4 tbsp milk

1 tbsp grated fresh ginger

2–3 bananas

about 4 tbsp golden syrup

♥ fireworks ♥

Remember, remember... give your guests plenty of notice as Bonfire Night is a popular night for a party!

Nature's invite
A conker invite captures the spirit of autumn. Plus it's easy and inexpensive to make but instantly gives that 'Wow' factor!

Who doesn't love a fireworks party? With that crisp, chilly air, autumn really lends itself to wrapping up, drinking a warming mug of something delicious and breathing in the smell of the bonfire. The weather might be windy and wild, but if you're prepared, it needn't dampen the fun. Umbrellas for people to shelter under to watch the fireworks display plus baskets full of extra gloves and scarves will keep everyone warm and cosy. The weather only really matters to the adults anyway – my son Sam says that the best party 'EVER' was the bonfire party where it poured with rain and everyone got stuck in the mud! Bonfire Night is also the perfect time to bring the garden inside. Leaves are at their most beautiful, berries are luscious, and there's an abundance of twigs, conkers and chestnuts – all of which are perfect for making gorgeous table centres. Use Harvest Festival as your inspiration, with gourds, peppers, oranges, lemons and limes providing a palette of bright, bold colours that zing against the night sky. There's something truly magical about watching a beautiful fireworks display in the freezing air, drinking cups of hot mulled wine, surrounded by friends and family. And it's even better if the air is filled with the heady scent of sausages sizzling! Six weeks in advance is a good time to send your invitations out to the most exciting party of the season. And how could your guests resist? It's going to be a blast!

Aim for the stars
Like your fireworks display, your table should be an explosion… of colourful treats piled high for your guests!

Shine a light
Torches are useful for guests mingling outside and also look brilliant all lit up in a basket!

Tasty toasties
Nothing says Bonfire Night quite like toasting marshmallows. Yum!

A cracking good invite (right)
Hang your conker invites from trees around your garden – the effect is fabulous!

Set taste buds alight (left)
Brightly coloured sweets will spark your guests' interest and their taste buds!

Be organized
Start collecting logs and branches from summer onwards, so by the time you host your fireworks party you have enough for an impressive bonfire.

All aglow
If, like me, you're not a fan of kids handling sparklers, fluorescent glow sticks and jewellery are a safe, fun alternative.

Sweet scent
The luscious scent of cinnamon in a warm glass of mulled wine is just divine.

Just for you (left)
Spoil your guests with a warming hot water bottle and delicious chocolates, to enjoy on the night and to take home. You could even attach a miniature bottle of whisky for adult guests.

Sparks fly (right)
Hand your guests an individual sparkling treat.

Special Occasion

flapjacks

it's the allspice that make these so special

TO MAKE THE FLAPJACKS

- Preheat the oven to 170°C/325°F/Gas 3. Line a 20cm/8in square tin with baking paper.
- In a large bowl, mix the oats, flour, sugar, allspice and salt together. Using your fingertips, break up any lumps of sugar so it is evenly dispersed.
- Put the butter and golden syrup in a saucepan and cook over a medium heat until melted. In a small bowl, dissolve the bicarbonate of soda in the boiling water. When the butter has melted, add the water mixture and stir continuously, until it begins to bubble and rise halfway up the sides of the pan.
- Pour the syrup mixture on top of the dry ingredients and mix well together. Spoon the mixture into the prepared tin and use a spatula or the back of a spoon to flatten the flapjack mixture.
- Bake in the oven for 15 minutes. Allow to cool in the tin for 10 minutes before cutting into squares, and then leave to cool completely in the tin to set.

MAKES	PREP/COOKING
16	20 mins/15 mins

INGREDIENTS

140g/5oz porridge oats

80g/3oz plain white flour

80g/3oz light brown muscovado sugar

½ tsp allspice

pinch of salt

80g/3oz unsalted butter

60g/2¼oz golden syrup

½ tsp bicarbonate of soda

2 tbsp boiling water

mulled wine
warming, aromatic and very more-ish

TO MAKE THE MULLED WINE
- Put all the ingredients in a large saucepan. Bring to the boil and simmer for 10–15 minutes, stirring occasionally, until the cranberries have popped and the sugar has dissolved.
- Serve in mugs, with a slice of orange on the edge, if wished.

SERVES	COOKING
6	10–15 mins

INGREDIENTS

1.2 litres/2 pints cranberry juice

1 cinnamon stick

2 cloves

50g/1¾oz fresh cranberries

50g/1¾oz sugar

¼ tsp ground cinnamon

1 orange, sliced (optional)

sticky sausages
simple but a sure-fire hit

TO MAKE THE SAUSAGES
- Preheat the oven to 200°C/400°F/Gas 6.
- Put the soy sauce, honey and mustard in a small bowl and stir well together.
- Put the sausages in a roasting tin and prick each one with a fork. Pour over the sauce and roll the sausages around to make sure they are all coated well in the sauce.
- Roast in the oven for 1 hour. Increase the oven temperature to 220°C/425°F/Gas 7 and cook for a further 30 minutes, until gloriously sticky and slightly burnt around the edges. If necessary, drain off any excess oil before serving.

SERVES	PREP/COOKING
8	10 mins/90 mins

INGREDIENTS

3 tbsp soy sauce

4 tbsp clear honey

3 tbsp wholegrain mustard

16 sausages

pocket rockets
a favourite with children of all ages

TO MAKE THE POCKET ROCKETS

- To make the marinade, put all the ingredients in a large bowl and stir well together until the sugar has dissolved.
- Cut the chicken into 2cm/¾in cubes. Add to the marinade, mix together and leave at room temperature for at least 30 minutes. Alternatively, leave to marinate in the refrigerator for 3–6 hours.
- Meanwhile, make the yogurt sauce. Crush the pink peppercorns with the salt. Add the yogurt and mix together. Turn into a serving bowl.
- Shred the lettuce hearts and put in a large serving bowl. Core and deseed the red peppers, dice the flesh and add to the lettuce. Sprinkle over the lemon juice.
- To serve, preheat the oven to 200°C/400°F/Gas 6. Heat the oil in a large saucepan over a high heat. Add the chicken and marinade juices and cook, stirring continuously, for 10 minutes. Transfer to a large serving bowl.
- Cut off the tops of the pitta breads lengthways and gently open the pockets. Warm the pitta breads in the oven for 3 minutes. Let your guests stuff the pocket rockets themselves with salad, chicken and a drizzle of the yogurt sauce.

MAKES

8

PREP & COOKING

30 mins (*plus marinating time*)

INGREDIENTS

12 skinless chicken breasts, organic/free-range

2 Romaine lettuce hearts

2 red peppers

juice of 1 lemon

2 tbsp olive or vegetable oil

12 large pitta breads

FOR THE MARINADE

6 tbsp finely chopped fresh rosemary

6 tbsp finely chopped fresh oregano

2–3 red chillies, deseeded and finely chopped

juice of 4 lemons

180ml/6fl oz soy sauce

3 garlic cloves, crushed

2 tbsp freshly grated fresh ginger

4 tbsp soft light brown sugar

FOR THE YOGURT SAUCE

4 tsp pink peppercorns

pinch of salt

600g/1 lb 5oz Greek yogurt

♥ valentine's supper ♥

*'Have some fun' is my motto for Valentine's Day!
Make it over-the-top romantic, so you can enjoy a
giggle together as well as eat something delicious.*

A basket of romance
*As this is a single, one-off invite, why not
really splash out, making a gift basket filled
with luxury treats? And then, of course,
you can enjoy hand-delivering it!*

A Valentine's supper is strictly a party for two… Going for a kitchen supper means it's less formal but doesn't mean you can't wow your loved one and make them feel special. But if I were to go for all-out, full on-romance on Valentine's, it would probably just make my husband Graham laugh. So I try to do something that indulges the romance of the occasion, but in a humorous, slightly over-the-top kind of way. Set the tone with your invite gift basket, topped with a lip-shaped tag that invites them to 'Meet you in the kitchen at 8.00pm'. It lets them know they are in for a fun, romantic evening. Take your pick from the wealth of Valentine's goodies available, from rose petals to heady floral scented candles to, if you are like me, heart-shaped anything and everything! I like a traditional colour scheme of white with daring splashes of red and some well-placed classic silver accessories. This is also the perfect opportunity to play all 'your' special songs. Why not make a Valentine's CD for your special someone, or prepare a Valentine's playlist? Once you've lovingly set the scene, your simple but gorgeously special three-course supper can be centre stage… along with you and your partner, of course!

Love at first sight

Alongside the scented candles and rose petals, include a favourite photograph of the two of you as part of your table decor.

Simple & bold
I love that contrast of classic, chic white table linen and really dramatic red accessories.

A good heart *(left)*
Heart-shaped doesn't have to be tacky – it can be romantic and beautiful.

Hand-delivered *(right)*
Champagne, strawberries, chocolate hearts… packaged with style and delivered with love.

Love letters
I don't think there's anything wrong with declaring what's on your mind!

Roses are red
Whether your budget stretches to bunches or just single stems, roses are the classic must-have flower for Valentine's.

Lipstick kisses
If you prefer a cheekier, more humorous approach, why not go for a paper tablecloth that you can adorn with your own personal lipstick messages?

Cheers *(right)*
Champagne on ice is a must for any Valentine's celebration. Either go for one large bottle or two miniatures as a sweet alternative.

I promise *(left)*
…'To love you for ever'. A 'Promise Voucher' makes your loved one feel special and promises to give them something they really want.

Promise Voucher

I promise to run you a bubble bath

Blooming decadent
Valentine's is the perfect occasion for making an extravagant statement with flamboyant flowers.

There's nothing sweeter than greeting your loved one with a ready glass of bubbly.

love heart bruschetta
made with love

TO MAKE THE BRUSCHETTA

- Preheat the grill to medium. Using a 7cm/2¾in heart-shaped cutter, cut out 1 heart per ciabatta slice, discarding the trimmings. Brush the heart-shaped slices with 1 tablespoon of the olive oil and toast under the grill for 2–3 minutes until golden on both sides.
- While the toast is still warm, take a handful of fresh basil and rub it into the toast. Cut the garlic in half and, cut side down, rub it into the toast. Set aside and leave to cool.
- Put the tomatoes in a saucepan of boiling water and blanch for 30 seconds–1 minute, but no longer or they will start to cook. Drain and remove the skin, which will now peel off easily. Cut each tomato into quarters and discard the seeds.
- Chop the tomato flesh into 1cm/½in pieces and put in a bowl. Finely chop the basil and add to the tomatoes with the remaining olive oil and the brown sugar. Season to taste with salt and pepper and mix well together. Leave at room temperature for 30 minutes, to marinate and allow the flavours to infuse.
- To serve, place 3 love-heart pieces of toast on each plate and spoon the tomato mixture on top. If using, rip the mozzarella or burrata over each bruschetta and add a few drops of olive oil around the plate and a grind of pepper.

SERVES
2

PREP & COOKING
30 mins *(plus marinating time)*

INGREDIENTS

6 slices ciabatta, about 1cm/½in thick

2 tbsp extra virgin olive oil

2 handfuls of fresh basil

1 garlic clove

4 ripe vine tomatoes

1 tsp brown sugar

1 ball buffalo mozzarella or burrata cheese (optional)

salt and freshly ground black pepper

balsamic marinated steak

serve on a bed of green leaves

TO MAKE THE STEAK

- ♥ Take the steaks out of the refrigerator at least 1 hour before you start to prepare the marinade.
- ♥ In a shallow bowl, combine the olive oil, balsamic vinegar, crushed garlic, lemon zest, pepper and sea salt and mix well together.
- ♥ Turn the steaks in the marinade to coat each side really well and leave to marinate for at least 1 hour in a cool place but not in the refrigerator. Alternatively, you can marinate the steaks, covered, for up to 12 hours in the refrigerator.
- ♥ To cook, preheat a frying pan or griddle over a high heat. When the pan is smoking hot, add the steaks, and cook for the required length of time, according to your taste. For a rare steak, cook for 2 minutes each side and allow to rest for 6 minutes. For a medium steak, cook for 3 minutes each side and allow to rest for 5 minutes. For a well-done steak, cook for 4 minutes each side and serve immediately on a warmed plate, without allowing any resting time.

SERVES	PREP/COOKING
2	30 mins/4–8 mins *(plus marinating time)*

INGREDIENTS

2 fillet steaks, 3–4cm/1–1½in thick

3 tbsp extra virgin olive oil

3 tbsp balsamic vinegar

1 garlic clove, crushed

grated zest of ½ lemon

1 tsp freshly ground black pepper

pinch of sea salt

creamy mash

a rich and indulgent treat

TO MAKE THE MASH

- ♥ Peel the potatoes and cut into large chunks. Put into a saucepan of water, bring to the boil and simmer for 15–20 minutes, until tender. Drain well and return to the pan.
- ♥ Add the butter and cream and mash together with a potato masher until smooth. Season to taste with salt and pepper, and serve with the steaks.

SERVES	PREP & COOKING
2	25–30 mins

INGREDIENTS

400g/14oz King Edward or Maris Piper potatoes

25g/1oz unsalted butter

4 tbsp double cream

salt and freshly ground black pepper

Special Occasion

indulgent chocolate mousse
serve with a kiss

TO MAKE THE MOUSSE

- Break the chocolate into pieces and put in a heatproof bowl set over a saucepan of simmering water. Heat gently until melted. When melted, stir until smooth and glossy. Remove the bowl from the pan and allow the chocolate to cool slightly.
- Whisk the egg whites until they stand in soft peaks and then add 1 tablespoon of sugar and whisk again. Continue until all the sugar has been incorporated and the egg whites are stiff and glossy.
- In a large bowl, whisk the cream until stiff. Using a large metal spoon, fold in the cooled chocolate followed by the egg whites.
- Spoon the chocolate mousse into serving bowls, martini glasses or espresso cups. Chill in the refrigerator for at least 1 hour before serving. Serve with heart-shaped chocolates.

SERVES
2

PREP/CHILLING
20 mins/1 hour

INGREDIENTS

85g/3oz dark chocolate
(minimum 70% cocoa solids)
2 egg whites
45g/1½oz caster sugar
150ml/¼ pint double cream
heart-shaped chocolates, to serve

♥ independence day ♥

I'm a real fan of 'Americana', whether it's white picket fences, New York cheesecake or that fantastic ability to really celebrate, big style!

Say it loud
Go for a visually arresting, iconic postcard invite that leaves your guests in no doubt that they've been invited to a big bonanza of a party!

Make no mistake, an Independence Day party is not just restricted to the good old 4th of July! With a little tweaking, the patriotic red, white and blue colour theme and styling works brilliantly for any large, legendary event that is worth celebrating. Maybe it's a major sporting final, or a once-in-a-generation historical occasion that provides the ideal opportunity to throw a big, big party. It's all about opening your doors and welcoming friends, family and neighbours to your home for great food and a fun time. It's an opportunity to be really bold, and to make an impact, so don't hold back on the fabulously strong red, white and blue colour scheme. Go mad with masses of red, white and blue balloons, bunting, streamers and table accessories. Fly a flag or two, either from a flagpole or simply draped over furniture. Load up buckets with more-ish popcorn, pretzels and sweets for your guests to dip into. And whether or not it's Independence Day, your tasty American-inspired menu of meatloaf hamburgers and miniature New York cheesecakes and chocolate brownies is sure to be a massive cause for celebration!

Bandanna style

A selection of red, white and blue bandannas make a fun and eye-catching alternative to a tablecloth!

Popping home *(left)*
Popcorn in a drawstring net bag with a customized label makes a cheap and fun take-home treat for your guests.

This party needs you *(right)*
Go for a selection of red, white and blue envelopes to send out your attention-grabbing invites.

Pick a pretzel
Serving pretzels in cute individual rolled-down paper bags is so much more interesting than just tipping them into a big bowl.

WE WANT YOU TO JOIN US AT OUR CELEBRATION PARTY!
SATURDAY 4TH JULY
70 GARDEN SQUARE, LONDON W8
FROM 6PM UNTIL MIDNIGHT
PREPARE FOR FOOD, DRINK, JOY & JUBILATIONS
RSVP: 07890 974 5467

Especially for you
Sweets with customized messages are always a big hit with your guests, and a little detail that shows you've put in that extra bit of thought and effort.

Don't blow it
If you're going for masses of balloons, it's always worth hiring a gas cylinder to make life easier!

Big on bunting *(right)*
There's nothing like loads of bunting to create a celebratory mood! Large flags look great too, draped over chairs and tables.

Customized treat *(left)*
If you'd really like to spoil your guests, how about a jar of tasty chutney to take home? Sporting a natty red, white and blue bandanna, of course!

And relax
If you're throwing a big party, it's always good to offer your guests the odd quiet haven to escape to, decorated in theme, of course.

WE THANK YOU FOR COMING TO OUR CELEBRATION

Special Occasion

Mini meatloaf hamburgers
made as a meatloaf, this is less hassle to make than individual burgers

TO MAKE THE HAMBURGERS

- Preheat the oven to 200°C/400°F/Gas 6. Line a large baking tray with baking paper.
- In a food processor or by hand, very finely chop the onion and blend together with the breadcrumbs and parsley. Grate the cheese and set aside.
- In a large bowl, combine the minced beef, eggs, tomato purée and ketchup, Worcestershire sauce, and the salt and pepper to taste. Add the breadcrumb mixture and mix and squash well together with your hands so that the flavours and consistency are even throughout.
- When everything has been sufficiently mixed together, put the mixture on the baking sheet and shape into a rectangle measuring 15–20cm/6–8in long, about 10cm/4in wide and 6cm/2½in high.
- Bake in the oven for 20 minutes, then remove from the oven, drizzle more ketchup over the top and sprinkle over the grated cheese.
- Bake for a further 10 minutes, until the cheese is melted and bubbling.
- To serve, cut into slices and put in hamburger buns or lightly toasted challah bread slices, with some lettuce, sliced red onion, tomatoes and gherkins. These are also delicious served cold the following day, and ideal for children's lunch boxes.

SERVES
6–8

PREP/COOKING
15 mins/30 mins

INGREDIENTS

1 onion

3 slices bread, made into breadcrumbs

2 tbsp finely chopped fresh flat-leaf parsley

50g/2oz Cheddar cheese

450g/1lb lean minced beef

3 medium eggs

1 tbsp tomato purée

3 tbsp tomato ketchup, plus extra to finish

½ tbsp Worcestershire sauce

2 tsp salt

freshly ground black pepper

TO SERVE

6–8 hamburger buns or 12–16 slices challah bread

shredded lettuce

thinly sliced red onion

sliced tomatoes

sliced gherkins

caesar salad

light and refreshing, the perfect accompaniment to the hamburgers

TO MAKE THE CAESAR SALAD

- ♥ First make the dressing. Put the lemon juice, sugar and salt in a large bowl and mix together until the sugar has dissolved. Whisk in the mayonnaise until smooth. Add the olive oil, season to taste with pepper and whisk again until all the ingredients have amalgamated.
- ♥ Cut the Romaine lettuce hearts into 2cm/¾in slices and separate the leaves. Add to the dressing and mix together until all the leaves are well coated. Add the grated Parmesan and gently stir.
- ♥ Remove the outer leaves from the Little Gem lettuces, wash and pat dry. Place the leaves, individually, on a serving plate and fill each leaf with 1–2 tablespoons of the dressed Romaine lettuce.
- ♥ If wished, garnish with Parmesan shavings and a little extra ground black pepper.

SERVES	PREP
6	15 mins

INGREDIENTS

juice of 2 lemons

2 tsp caster sugar

½ tsp salt

4 tbsp mayonnaise

8 tbsp extra virgin olive oil

2 Romaine lettuce hearts

2 tbsp coarsely grated Parmesan cheese

4 Little Gem lettuces

3 tbsp Parmesan shavings (optional)

freshly ground black pepper

Independence Day

Special Occasion

miniature cheesecakes
serve in muffin wraps to make these easier for your guests to eat

TO MAKE THE CHEESECAKES

- ♥ Preheat the oven to 180°C/350°F/Gas 4. Line 2 12-hole muffin tins with 22 paper cases.
- ♥ Put the biscuits in a large bowl or strong polythene bag and crush with the end of a wooden rolling pin to form fine breadcrumbs. Alternatively, blitz in a food processor until finely crushed.
- ♥ Melt the butter, then add to the biscuit crumbs and mix well together. Divide the mixture equally between the paper cases and press down well with your fingers. Put in the refrigerator and leave to set while you make the topping.
- ♥ To make the topping, put the cream cheese and sugar in a large bowl and whisk together until light and fluffy. Add the eggs and vanilla extract and beat together until completely smooth. Divide the topping evenly between the paper cases.
- ♥ Bake in the oven for 30–35 minutes, until lightly golden on top. Leave the cheesecakes in the tins for 20 minutes, and then transfer to a wire rack and leave to cool.
- ♥ Meanwhile, make the coulis. Put all the ingredients in a food processor and blitz until the sauce is smooth. Alternatively, put all the ingredients in a bowl and mash together with a fork. Press the sauce through a sieve with the back of a wooden spoon.
- ♥ To serve, very thinly slice the strawberries. Put a little coulis on the top of each cheesecake and decorate with the sliced strawberries. If you've any leftover coulis, drizzle this over vanilla ice cream or yogurt – it makes a delicious sweet treat!

MAKES
24

PREP/COOKING
30 mins/30–35 mins

INGREDIENTS
200g/7oz digestive biscuits
140g/5oz butter
650g/1lb 7oz full-fat soft
  cream cheese
150g/5½oz caster sugar
3 medium eggs
½ tsp vanilla extract
strawberries, to serve

FOR THE COULIS
270g/9½oz strawberries, hulled
30g/1oz caster sugar
2 tsp lemon juice

brownies

best made the day before you want to serve them

TO MAKE THE BROWNIES

- ♥ Preheat the oven to 170°C/325°F/Gas 3. Line a shallow 20cm/8in square brownie tin with baking paper.
- ♥ Break the chocolate into pieces and put in a heatproof bowl set over a saucepan of simmering water. Add the butter, cut into small pieces and heat until melted. When melted, stir until smooth and glossy and then add the sugar. Remove the bowl from the pan and allow the chocolate to cool slightly.
- ♥ Meanwhile, in an electric mixer, or using a large mixing bowl and an electric hand-held mixer, whisk the eggs together until light and fluffy.
- ♥ Add the cooled chocolate mixture to the eggs and gently stir until incorporated. Sift in the plain flour and self-raising flour, and then fold into the mixture.
- ♥ When the mixture is smooth, fold in the chocolate chips and pour the mixture into the prepared tin.
- ♥ Bake in the oven for 35 minutes, until the top is set enough to the touch. Leave in the tin to cool completely. When cold, cover with clingfilm to keep fresh overnight.
- ♥ To serve, remove the whole brownie square from the tin. Peel away the baking paper and cut into 25 little brownies. Serve dusted with sifted icing sugar. These are very rich so it's perfect just to have small mouthfuls of chocolate heaven!

MAKES	PREP/COOKING
25	20 mins/35 mins

INGREDIENTS

275g/9½oz dark chocolate
  (minimum 70% cocoa solids)
275g/9½oz unsalted butter
325g/11½oz golden caster sugar
4 medium eggs
125g/4½oz plain white flour
50g/1¾oz self-raising flour
50g/1¾oz white chocolate chips
50g/1¾oz milk chocolate chips
icing sugar, for dusting

♥ afternoon tea ♥

A vintage tea party is an old and trusted favourite of mine that is suitable for many different occasions.

Teatime taster
Gorgeous tea bags, the ones made out of delicate gauze, with a pretty customized label, perfectly set the tone for an afternoon of unashamedly traditional treats.

The essential elements of this tea party are so simple and yet the overall effect is totally glorious. It's all about creating a really eclectic, pretty, old-fashioned mix. Go for mismatched china teapots, dainty cups and saucers and faded floral tablecloths in a soft pastel palette. Add in the scent of lavender and you can easily create the setting of a gentler time, when elegant ladies in hats and gloves enjoyed a quiet chat over afternoon tea. Equally suited to an indoor or outdoor setting, a mismatch of chintzy prints works wonderfully with pretty antique silver items. You may already have plenty of lovely china – or if not, your mother or grandmother may some hidden away somewhere! Flowers make a beautiful focal point to the vintage theme. Use traditional flowers such as chrysanthemums, peonies, freesias and sweet peas in gentle pinks, whites and lilacs to achieve that 'English country garden' look. Add in a cake stand laden with zesty lemon squares and yummy iced biscuits, and afternoon tea is ready to be served!

Just for you
With its fabulously feminine, retro feel, a vintage tea party is perfect for Mother's Day. I've also prepared this as a special birthday treat for my mother.

It's the thought that counts
Customize tiny jam jars with cute little fabric tops and sweet messages. Guests will feel extra special when tucking in!

One lump or two...

Silver treasures (left)
Nothing captures that 'old-fashioned tea room' feel like tiny silver bells and antique tea strainers.

Time for tea (right)
Why not have a range of speciality and traditional teas that your guests can enjoy sampling?

Delicately beautiful
Choose flowers such as peonies and clematis and sprigs of lavender to create a gentle wash of soft colours.

You are invited to a
Vintage Afternoon Tea Party
~ a perfect blend ~
Sunday 23 August
3 o'clock
4 The Cloisters
London
RSVP
020 7 329 678 90

Especially for you
A china cup and saucer, prettily wrapped, makes a lovely take-home gift for your guests.

Treasure hunt
Car boot sales, junk shops and charity shops are all great for one-off vintage finds that bring colour and personality to your decor.

Little touches (right)
Individual flower heads in gorgeous teacups, sugar bowls and milk jugs look amazing.

Mmmmm, yes please (left)
Rather than large single cakes, go for dainty cake stands offering lots of delicious smaller treats, so your guests can enjoy trying a few without feeling too guilty!

Tea for you
Have some charming little boxes and ribbons handy so your guests can take away samples of any of the teas they have particularly enjoyed on the day.

Chequerboard styling
*Display your sandwiches
alternately to create a fabulous
chequerboard effect.*

smoked mackerel pâté open sandwiches
the beetroot adds a sweet flavour

TO MAKE THE PÂTÉ SANDWICHES

- Remove the skin from the mackerel fillets and flake the fish into small pieces into a bowl. Add the cream cheese and mix with a fork until it is a smooth consistency.
- Add the crème fraîche, mustard, lemon juice and 1 tablespoon of the chopped parsley.
- To serve, thinly slice the beetroot and then it cut into 5mm/¼in cubes. Slice the challah bread into 1cm/½in thick slices (depending on the size of the loaf, you'll need about 12 slices) and remove the crusts. Cut the bread slices into 4cm/1½in squares.
- Spoon 1 teaspoon of the mackerel pâté onto each square. Top with 3 beetroot cubes, a pinch of the remaining chopped parsley and lastly, a sprinkle of lemon zest.

SERVES	PREP
6	25 mins

INGREDIENTS

75g/2¾oz smoked peppered mackerel

40g/1½oz full-fat soft cream cheese

2 tbsp crème fraîche

1 tsp wholegrain English mustard

grated zest and juice of 1 lemon

2 tbsp finely chopped fresh flat-leaf parsley

100g/3½oz cooked beetroot

challah bread, to serve

cucumber cream cheese open sandwiches
light, delicate and refreshing

TO MAKE THE CREAM CHEESE SANDWICHES

- Put the cream cheese and crème fraîche in a bowl and beat together until smooth. Add the dill and season with a pinch of salt. Set aside.
- Peel and deseed the cucumber. Cut the prepared cucumber into very fine strips then cut each piece into very small cubes, about 3mm/⅛in square. Set aside.
- Slice the radishes into fine strands. You just need a few strands for each piece of bread.
- To serve, slice the soda bread into 1cm/½in thick slices (depending on the size of the loaf, you'll need about 12 slices) and remove the crusts. Cut the bread slices into 4cm/1½in squares.
- Spoon half a teaspoon of the cream cheese mixture onto each square. Top with a few cucumber cubes, and then a couple of strands of the chopped radish.

SERVES	PREP
6	25 mins

INGREDIENTS

75g/2¾oz full-fat soft cream cheese

1 tbsp crème fraîche

½ tsp very finely chopped fresh dill

½ cucumber

2 radishes

salt

soda bread, to serve

lemon squares
a wonderfully zesty treat

TO MAKE THE LEMON SQUARES

- Preheat the oven to 180°C/350°F/Gas 4. Line a shallow 20cm/ 8in square cake tin with baking paper.
- To make the base, in an electric mixer, or using a large mixing bowl and an electric hand-held mixer, cream the butter and sugar together.
- Add the flour and then the milk and mix together until smooth. Spoon the mixture into the prepared tin, spreading it over the base and working it into the corners of the tin.
- Bake in the oven for 15 minutes.
- Meanwhile, make the topping. In a clean electric mixer or another bowl, whisk the eggs and sugar together until light and fluffy. Add the lemon zest and juice and then fold in the flour.
- Remove the cooked bottom layer from the oven and spoon the lemon mixture on top. Return to the oven and bake for a further 15 minutes, until golden. Leave in the tin to cool completely.
- To serve, cut into 16 squares and dust with sifted icing sugar.

MAKES	PREP/COOKING
16	15 mins/30 mins

FOR THE BASE

100g/3½oz unsalted butter,
  at room temperature
40g/1½oz icing sugar
150g/5½oz plain white flour
3 tbsp milk

FOR THE TOPPING

3 medium eggs
220g/7¾oz caster sugar
grated zest of 2 lemons and juice
  of 1 lemon
40g/1½oz plain white flour
icing sugar, for dusting

Vintage

fruit scones

a traditional tasty treat

TO MAKE THE SCONES

- ♥ Preheat the oven to 220°C/425°F/Gas 7. Line a baking tray with baking paper.
- ♥ In a large bowl, sift the flour, cream of tartar, bicarbonate of soda and salt together. Stir in the sugar.
- ♥ Add the butter to the flour and rub in until the mixture resembles fine breadcrumbs. Make a well in the centre.
- ♥ Whisk the buttermilk and 2 of the eggs together. Pour into the well in the flour mixture and, stirring from the centre and working outwards, stir in the flour until combined. Add the raisins and mix into the dough.
- ♥ Turn out the dough onto a lightly floured surface and knead gently, adding a little extra flour if the dough is too wet and sticky. Roll out the dough to about 3cm/1¼in thickness.
- ♥ Dip a 5cm/2in fluted round cutter in flour before cutting each scone (this will help to make perfect fluted-edged scones). Cut out 12 rounds and place the scones on the prepared baking tray. Whisk the remaining egg and use to brush the tops of each scone, to glaze.
- ♥ Bake in the oven for 6–8 minutes, until golden. Serve with clotted cream, strawberry conserve and sliced fresh strawberries.

MAKES	PREP/COOKING
12	20 mins/6–8 mins

INGREDIENTS

350g/12oz self-raising flour, plus extra for dusting

2 tsp cream of tartar

2 tsp bicarbonate of soda

½ tsp salt

70g/2½oz caster sugar

75g/2¾oz cold unsalted butter, diced

100ml/3½fl oz buttermilk

3 medium eggs

60g/2¼oz raisins

TO SERVE

clotted cream

strawberry conserve

fresh strawberries, sliced

spiced teatime biscuits
sugar flowers look and taste so sweet

TO MAKE THE BISCUITS

- Preheat the oven to 180°C/350°F/Gas 4. Line 2 large baking trays with baking paper.
- In an electric mixer, or using a large mixing bowl and an electric hand-held mixer, cream the butter and sugar together until light and fluffy, and then beat in the egg.
- Sift the flour, baking powder, salt, nutmeg and allspice into another bowl and mix together. Add 2 tablespoons at a time to the butter mixture, stirring continually until all the flour is incorporated. If the biscuit mixture looks very sticky at this point, add another tablespoon of flour and mix in well.
- Bring the dough into a ball and wrap in clingfilm. Put in the refrigerator for at least 30 minutes to allow the dough to rest and slightly harden.
- Dust the work surface and rolling pin with flour and roll out the dough to about 5mm/¼in thickness. Using a 6cm/2½in fluted cutter, or your desired shapes, letters or numbers, cut out the dough and place on the prepared baking trays.
- Bake in the oven for 6–8 minutes, until the biscuits are golden. Transfer to a wire rack and leave to cool completely before icing.
- When the biscuits are cold, make the icing. Sift the icing sugar into a large bowl and add enough water to make a thick, smooth icing. Dip a skewer into the food colouring and then stir into the icing to colour.
- Using a teaspoon, spread the icing on top of the biscuits and smooth over. Decorate with sugar flowers and leave to set.

MAKES	PREP/COOKING
26–28	45 mins/6–8 mins
	(plus chilling and cooling time)

INGREDIENTS

90g/3¼oz unsalted butter,
   at room temperature
100g/3½oz light brown
   muscovado sugar
1 medium egg
200g/7oz plain white flour,
   plus extra for dusting
½ tsp baking powder
½ tsp salt
¼ tsp ground nutmeg
¼ tsp allspice
edible sugar flowers, to decorate

FOR THE ICING

300g/10¼oz icing sugar
4–5 tsp water
mauve food colouring

♥ black & white party ♥

Chic, classic and sophisticated... how I'd sum up my perfect cocktail party!

I spy
A stylish eye mask sent in a luxurious black box has the 'wow' factor and leaves your guests in no doubt that they are coming to a really special event!

Black and white has amazing potential for a party theme. Personally, I take my lead from classic Hollywood movies such as *Manhattan* and *Brief Encounter*, and am inspired by the elegance of such films as *Breakfast at Tiffany's*. Keep the sophistication of Audrey Hepburn and the charm of the Rat Pack in mind, and you can't go wrong. Black and white gives you a strong background on which to add stylish accessories, such as gorgeous white roses in black vases and strings of pearls. Flower-wise, individual cut-down white roses in black vases look particularly elegant, and a mass of over-sized white blooms in a huge black vase looks fabulously dramatic. Music really helps set the mood. Go for classic jazz or Dean Martin or, to make a real impact, a live swing band to get people dancing! This party is very much about the grown-ups, but you could easily adapt it for an eighteenth birthday party. Add in mirror balls and a black and white dance floor and you have something that works for younger guests. Food-wise, it's about stand-up rather than sit-down. 'Cocktail eats' that can be enjoyed with one hand while mingling and holding a glass in the other are on the menu for this very special evening.

Cocktails at Tiffany's
For one night only, take out your family snaps and replace them with classic black-and-white photographs of some of the Hollywood greats, like the beautiful Audrey Hepburn.

Enjoy the elegance
*It's definitely grown-up time…
with cocktails, chic table
accessories and Sinatra
playing in the background.*

Back to vinyl
A selection of classic albums will grab your guests' interest and provide a great talking point for the evening.

White stuff *(left)*
Beautiful white chrysanthemums, roses or orchids in glossy black vases are simple yet striking.

Indulgent treats *(right)*
Jars of black-and-white sweets or fluffy white marshmallows make a strong visual impact as well as tempting your guests to tuck in!

Sophisticated treats
Black licorice sticks in heavy glass jars make fabulous eye candy!

Mood lighting
Masses of candles are the way to go. Use large church candles as a centrepiece for your table, with smaller ones dotted round to create atmosphere.

Contrasting colours
Go for black and white bowls, black and white napkins, black and white candles… and anything else you can think of!

Just for you *(right)*
A bundle of gorgeous vintage black-and-white postcards tied with chic ribbon make a great memento of the evening, and are something that your guests can enjoy using.

Extra special *(left)*
Add depth to the stark black and white colour scheme with some carefully selected silver pieces.

corn on the cob soup

so fabulously creamy, one shot is never enough

TO MAKE THE SOUP

- Remove the kernels from the corn on the cobs. Finely chop the onions and celery sticks. Crush the garlic.
- Heat the oil and butter in a large saucepan over a low heat, until the butter has melted. Add the onions, celery, garlic and a pinch of salt, stir and cook over a low heat for 5–10 minutes, until the onions are softened but not browned.
- Add the corn kernels and then pour in 800ml/28fl oz of stock and season to taste with pepper. Cover the pan with a lid and simmer for 15–20 minutes, until the corn is tender.
- Remove from the heat and allow to cool slightly. Pour into a blender, or use a hand-held blender, and blitz until smooth. Add the double cream and blitz again. If the soup is too thick, add a little extra stock until it is the consistency that you like.
- Chill in the refrigerator for 2–3 hours, or overnight. Serve in tall shot glasses.
- If wished, serve with slices of ciabatta, brushed with a little olive oil and toasted in the oven at 170°C/325°F/Gas 3 for about 15 minutes, turning once, until golden.

SERVES	PREP/CHILLING
12	35–45 mins/
	2–3 hours

INGREDIENTS

2 corn on the cobs

2 small onions

2 celery sticks

1 garlic clove

1 tbsp olive oil

a knob of unsalted butter

800–900ml/28–31fl oz
   vegetable stock

2 tbsp double cream

salt and freshly ground
   black pepper

TO SERVE (OPTIONAL)

ciabatta bread

olive oil

beetroot and thyme soup

the beetroot gives this soup the most divine colour

TO MAKE THE SOUP

- Roughly chop the beetroot, reserving the water it is packed in. Cut the carrot into small dice. Finely chop the onion and garlic.
- Heat the oil in a large saucepan. Add the onion and fry over a low heat for about 5 minutes until translucent but not brown, so keep a close watch on it. Add the garlic and carrot to the pan and fry for a further 2–3 minutes, stirring occasionally to make sure nothing is catching on the bottom of the pan.
- Add the beetroot, the leaves from the sprigs of thyme and 600ml/1 pint of the stock to the pan. Stir and simmer over a low heat for 15 minutes. Add the cream and season to taste with salt and pepper.
- Leave to cool slightly and then pour into a blender and purée to a smooth consistency. If necessary, add a little more stock to thin the soup.
- Chill in the refrigerator for 2–3 hours, or overnight. You may find after chilling that the soup is slightly thicker and loses some of its vibrancy; add a couple of tablespoons of the reserved beetroot water to thin it and restore its punchy colour. Serve in tall shot glasses.
- If wished, serve with slices of ciabatta, brushed with a little olive oil and toasted in the oven at 170°C/325°F/Gas 3 for about 15 minutes, turning once, until golden.

SERVES	PREP/CHILLING
12	40 mins/2–3 hours

INGREDIENTS

500g/1lb 2oz cooked beetroot, packed in water

1 carrot

1 onion

2 garlic cloves

1 tbsp olive oil

2 large sprigs fresh thyme

600–800ml/1 pint–28½fl oz chicken or vegetable stock

2 tbsp double cream

salt and freshly ground black pepper

TO SERVE (OPTIONAL)

ciabatta bread

olive oil

cucumber and dill soup
garnish with a delicate swirl of crème fraîche

TO MAKE THE SOUP

- Slice the onions. Cut the potatoes into large chunks. Peel and deseed the cucumbers and cut into cubes.
- Melt the butter in a large saucepan, add the onions and cook over a low heat for about 5 minutes, until softened but not browned. Add the potato and 800ml/28fl oz of stock, bring to a boil and simmer for 8–10 minutes until the potato is almost cooked.
- Add the cucumbers and simmer for 2–3 minutes. Remove from the heat and stir in the chopped dill.
- Pour into a blender and purée until smooth. If the soup is too thick, add the remaining stock until it is the right consistency. Season to taste with salt and pepper.
- Chill in the refrigerator for 2–3 hours, or overnight.
- Serve the soup in tall shot glasses, garnished with a swirl of crème fraîche and/or a little chopped dill, if wished.
- If wished, serve with slices of ciabatta, brushed with a little olive oil and toasted in the oven at 170°C/325°F/Gas 3 for about 15 minutes, turning once, until golden.

SERVES	PREP/CHILLING
12	35 mins/2–3 hours

INGREDIENTS

2 onions

1 large, floury potato

2 cucumbers

50g/1¾oz unsalted butter

800ml–1 litre/28fl oz–1¾ pints
   chicken or vegetable stock

2 tsp finely chopped fresh dill plus
   extra, to garnish (optional)

crème fraîche, to garnish
   (optional)

salt and freshly ground
   black pepper

TO SERVE (OPTIONAL)

ciabatta bread

olive oil

Simply stunning
Serve your soups in tall shot glasses, accompanied by slithers of toasted ciabatta. Simple, chic but so effective.

nutmeg chocolate truffles

the darker the chocolate, the more yummy these taste

TO MAKE THE TRUFFLES

- ♥ Break the chocolate into small chunks and put into a blender. Blend to a fine powder and then place in a large mixing bowl.
- ♥ Put the cream and nutmeg in a saucepan and heat to just before it reaches boiling point, to infuse the flavour. Remove from the heat.
- ♥ Add 2 dessertspoons of the nutmeg cream to the chocolate and stir until completely amalgamated. Add another 2 dessertspoons of cream, stir and repeat until all the cream has been incorporated. This slow process is important in order to prevent the mixture from splitting.
- ♥ When all the cream has been incorporated, add a small piece of butter and mix well. Keep adding the butter, one small piece at a time, until the mixture is silky smooth. Chill the mixture in the refrigerator for at least 3 hours, until firm.
- ♥ When the truffle mixture is set, chop the flaked almonds on a large board. Using a teaspoon, scoop out rounds of truffle mixture and gently roll in the palms of your hands.
- ♥ Gently roll the truffles in the chopped almonds to coat. (Work quickly and lightly with your hands to prevent the mixture from melting.) Place in the refrigerator to set again before serving.

MAKES	PREP/CHILLING
About 75	40 mins/3 hours

INGREDIENTS

550g/1lb 4oz dark chocolate
   (minimum 70% cocoa solids)
525ml/19fl oz double cream
1 tsp grated nutmeg
125g/4½oz unsalted butter,
   at room temperature
200g/7oz flaked almonds

white chocolate cinnamon & raisin truffles

it's the hint of cinnamon with the raisin that really makes these

TO MAKE THE TRUFFLES

- ♥ Break the chocolate into small chunks and put into a blender. Blend to a fine powder then place in a large mixing bowl.
- ♥ Put the cream and cinnamon in a saucepan and heat to just before it reaches boiling point, to infuse the flavour. Remove from the heat.
- ♥ Add 2 dessertspoons of the cinnamon cream to the chocolate, stir in and repeat until all the cream has been added.
- ♥ When all the cream has been incorporated, add a small piece of butter and mix well. Keep adding the butter, one small piece at a time, until all the butter has been added. Fold in the raisins. Chill the mixture in the refrigerator for at least 3 hours, until firm.
- ♥ When the truffle mixture is set, chop the flaked almonds on a large board. Using a teaspoon, scoop out rounds of truffle mixture and gently roll in the palms of your hands.
- ♥ Gently roll the truffles in the chopped almonds to coat. (Work quickly and lightly with your hands to prevent the mixture from melting.) Place in the refrigerator to set again before serving.

MAKES	PREP/CHILLING
About 75	40 mins/3 hours

INGREDIENTS

525g/1lb 3oz good-quality white chocolate

375ml/13fl oz double cream

1 tsp ground cinnamon

225g/8oz unsalted butter, at room temperature

200g/7oz raisins

200g/7oz flaked almonds

Vintage

Mountains of truffles
Yes, they may be decadent and indulgent, but be warned, your guests will keep coming back for more of these divine truffles!

♥ baby shower ♥

All the best baby showers are unashamedly girly – and a strictly man-free, child-free zone!

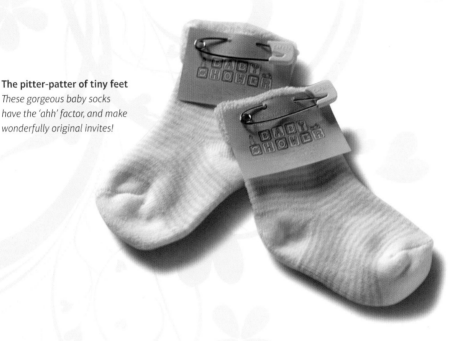

The pitter-patter of tiny feet
These gorgeous baby socks have the 'ahh' factor, and make wonderfully original invites!

A baby shower should be a double celebration – not only of the very special fact that a new baby is on the way, but also in recognition of the woman with the bump who deserves some serious spoiling before her life changes for ever. It's an opportunity to live out the baby dream, with divine little baby clothes and indulgent treats, and to chat among friends and really enjoy those last moments of peace and quiet before the joy, and the chaos, of having a tiny new baby in the home. Throw a baby shower at a time when the pregnant mummy is feeling her best – the 'nesting' period between seven and nine months is perfect. The star guest will be dying for something to do, impatient for the new arrival and thrilled to spend time with girlfriends. Find out what time of day she's feeling at her best – is she craving breakfast, lunch or tea? – and plan your party time and menu accordingly. The theming can be great fun and the options for adding pretty touches are endless. I personally am not keen on the 'gender neutral' lemon and would say nothing beats white, with splashes of pinks and blues. Go all-out for girly heaven, with pretty flowers decorating plates of yummy food and adorable baby trinkets as table decorations – you could even substitute traditional napkins for 'nappy-kins'! Most importantly of all, kick back, have fun and indulge your pregnant girlfriend. She deserves it.

All grown up
*Baby needn't mean babyish –
a few select baby items can
create a fun, stylish table with
heaps of personality.*

Baby Shower

Drink up

Baby bottles with straws are perfect for serving peach bellinis. You can also fill them with sweets for a charming take-home gift for your guests.

Blooming marvellous

Pink for a girl and blue for a boy...
go all-out for really pretty flowers
in soft pastels.

Sweet treat

Indulge in some seriously naughty
treats, such as dolly mixtures
and – my favourite – yummy mini
milk bottles.

Baby bunting (left)

Why not create unique bunting
from your beautiful baby sock
invites? Nothing could be sweeter!

Gorgeous miniatures (below)

Pieces of dolls' house furniture,
such as these old-fashioned
prams, make beautiful and
original decorations.

Mix it up

Get your colour palette right and
you can have fun mixing flowers
with cute toys and gorgeous one-
off pieces, like this amazing vintage
bird cage.

Nappy-kins

Fluffy white newborn-size
nappies, folded and fastened
with an old-fashioned nappy pin,
make an original napkin!

Whose shoes

I challenge any girl not to coo
over tiny baby shoes! They make
an adorable table decoration.

A is for

Cute building blocks are a witty
detail to add to your table. You
could use them to spell out
'CONGRATULATIONS' or 'BABY'.

Bib & tucker

Have fun with your accessories,
like these baby bibs draped over
the back of your guests' chairs.

Parents

salmon & watercress tartlets
delicious with a simple rocket salad

TO MAKE THE TARTLETS

- Preheat the oven to 180°C/350°F/Gas 4. Remove the pastry from the refrigerator 5 minutes before you begin cooking to make it easier to work with.
- Unroll the pastry and cut into 6 even-sized pieces. Use to line 6 10cm/4in diameter, 2cm/¼in deep loose-based tart tins. Use your fingertips to gently push the pastry into the bases and use a rolling pin to remove the excess from the tops. If any tears occur, patch them with a little of the leftover pastry. Place the lined tins on a baking tray.
- Sprinkle the watercress equally between the tins and then flake the salmon on top.
- Whisk the cream, egg and egg yolk together and season to taste with salt and pepper. Pour over the salmon and watercress, dividing it equally between the tins.
- Bake in the oven for 20 minutes, until set and lightly browned. Leave to cool for 5–10 minutes before removing from the tins. Serve hot, or cool on a wire rack and serve cold.

MAKES
6

PREP/COOKING
15 mins/20 mins

INGREDIENTS

375g packet ready-rolled shortcrust pastry

3 handfuls watercress, stalks removed

100g/3½oz smoked salmon, preferably hot smoked

150ml/¼ pint double cream

1 medium egg

1 egg yolk

salt and freshly ground black pepper

ginger & passion fruit fools

yummy served straight from the fridge

TO MAKE THE FOOLS

- ❤ Very finely chop the ginger and set aside.
- ❤ Cut the passion fruit in half, scoop out the flesh into a sieve and push through to extract the juice.
- ❤ In a large bowl, whisk the cream until it stands in soft peaks.
- ❤ Sift the icing sugar into a large bowl. Add the passion fruit juice and lemon juice and mix together, adding a further tablespoon of sifted icing sugar if the passion fruit are unripe and sour.
- ❤ Using a large metal spoon, gently fold the juice mixture, a spoonful at a time, into the whipped cream. Gently fold in the chopped crystallized ginger.
- ❤ Spoon the mixture into cocktail glasses and leave to set in the refrigerator for at least 2 hours.

SERVES	PREP/SETTING
6	25 mins/2 hours

INGREDIENTS

1 tbsp crystallized ginger

15 passion fruit

450ml/16fl oz double cream

100g/3½oz icing sugar

juice of ½ lemon

oatmeal & raisin cookies

perfect with a glass of cold milk

TO MAKE THE COOKIES

- ❤ Preheat the oven to 170°C/325°F/Gas 3. Line 3 large baking trays with baking parchment.
- ❤ Put the flour, oats, bicarbonate of soda, cinnamon, nutmeg and salt in a large bowl and mix together.
- ❤ In an electric mixer or a large bowl with a wooden spoon, cream the butter and sugar together until fluffy. Beat in the egg.
- ❤ Add the dry ingredients to the mixture a spoonful at a time until well mixed. Fold in the raisins.
- ❤ Using a teaspoon, spoon dollops of the cookie mixture onto the prepared baking trays, at least 4cm/1½in apart to allow room for spreading.
- ❤ Bake in the oven for 10–15 minutes, until golden brown around the edges and still soft in the centre. Transfer to a wire rack and leave to cool.

MAKES	PREP/COOKING
25–30	25 mins/10–15 mins

INGREDIENTS

190g/5¾oz plain white flour

50g/ 1¾oz porridge oats

½ tsp bicarbonate of soda

½ tsp ground cinnamon

½ tsp ground nutmeg

½ tsp salt

135g/4¾oz unsalted butter, softened

160g/5¾oz light brown muscovado sugar

1 medium egg

100g/3½oz raisins

Decorating a table for a
baby shower is definitely
my idea of a treat, rather
than a chore!

♥ fiesta ♥

*Just the word gets me in the party mood!
It says celebration, music, piñatas, streamers —
and most importantly, fun!*

Flamboyance & flair
*For the invite, set the mood of vibrant
but still sleek, with a dramatic black and
white postcard customized with feathers
and jewels in hot clashing colours.*

The great thing about a fiesta party is that its relaxed but lively vibe works for children, teens and adults. The one essential element is an outdoor space, which you can decorate to your heart's content. The colour scheme is a full-on explosion of colour – hot pinks, lime greens, zingy oranges and bright yellows. So go for fiery-coloured streamers hanging from the trees, red-hot ribbons wound round tree trunks, vibrant piñatas hanging from branches, and exotic birds and butterflies nestled in bushes. Invite your younger guests to delve into a popcorn-filled lucky dip, to discover brightly wrapped gifts of whistles and castanets. Cheap and cheerful prizes that really ramp up the noise level! And have some lively music playing – mariachi-style. Finally, get your guests into the party mood with exotic cocktails, served with as many clashing umbrellas and streamers as you can cram on to them. After all, more is definitely more when you're throwing a fiesta party!

Plastic and acrylic picnic-style accessories and contrasting paper napkins add to the bright and bold colour scheme. And if you can't find tablecloths in the perfect colours, simply use lengths of fabric.

Hanging around
Overload trees with vibrant decorations: a selection of streamers, beautiful glass tealight holders and really pretty lanterns.

Cheers
Have a selection of alcoholic and non-alcoholic treats for your guests to enjoy. Just make sure all are served in a suitably flamboyant fashion!

Dinner is served
A paper napkin and a plate are what your guests will be expecting – so add a party blower and tie up the bundle with string to make that bit more of a statement.

Interesting one-offs
Add interest and drama to your decor with a selection of fun, vibrant accessories.

Beautifully bold *(left)*
A painted plant pot in a clashing colour makes the perfect container for bright and beautiful flowers.

Tasty treat *(right)*
Monkey nuts in a sombrero-style striped paper cone can be eaten at the party or taken away to enjoy at home. Popcorn makes a great alternative if nuts are not suitable for all your guests.

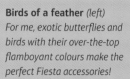

LA FIESTA!

BLOW YOUR WHISTLE AND BANG YOUR BONGOS AT

OUR FIESTA PARTY!

SATURDAY 23 AUGUST

50 OAK AVENUE
LONDON, NW8 2QG

JOIN US AT THE HOTTEST SPOT
NORTH OF HAVANA FROM 7PM TO 3AM
PLEASE RSVP TO LIVINLAVIDA @ BVS-LONDON.COM

Birds of a feather *(left)*
For me, exotic butterflies and birds with their over-the-top flamboyant colours make the perfect Fiesta accessories!

Shake, rattle & roll *(right)*
A selection of musical instruments for your guests to play is sure to raise both the volume and the party spirit!

Get your guests in the party
mood by playing hook-a-duck,
customized with feathers of
course! They can take their
fabulous duck home as a memento.

granita
sure to hit the spot, with or without the vodka

TO MAKE THE GRANITA
- ♥ Put the sugar and hot water in a cup and stir until the sugar has dissolved.
- ♥ In a blender, put the peaches, mango, grated zest and lime juice, ice, the sugar water and the vodka, if using to make an alcoholic version. Blitz until smooth.
- ♥ Pour into a freezerproof container and freeze for 2 hours. Mash with a fork to break up the ice particles and then return to the freezer for a further 2 hours. Mash again and then freeze for at least 1 hour, until firm or required. Cover the container with a lid for storing.

SERVES	PREP/FREEZING
6	10 mins/5 hours

INGREDIENTS
1 tbsp caster sugar

2 tbsp hot water

410g can peach halves in juice, drained

425g can mango in syrup, drained

grated zest and juice of 2 limes

1 cup ice

90ml/3¼fl oz vodka (optional)

jalapeño soured cream sauce
cool — and a bit spicy

TO MAKE THE SAUCE

- ♥ Finely chop the jalapeño peppers. Put the soured cream and yogurt in a bowl and mix together.
- ♥ Stir in the peppers and season with the salt. Transfer to a bowl to serve.

SERVES	PREP
6	5 mins

INGREDIENTS

30g/1¼oz jalapeño peppers, drained (if you prefer a milder sauce, you may prefer to reduce the quantity of jalapeños to 15g/½oz)

300ml/½ pint soured cream

2 tbsp Greek yogurt

pinch of salt

guacamole
tangy and creamy

TO MAKE THE GUACAMOLE

- ♥ Put the lemon juice and oil in a medium bowl. Skin and stone the avocados and cut into chunks. Add to the bowl and, using a fork, mash until smooth.
- ♥ Core, deseed and very finely chop the red peppers. Finely chop the coriander. Stir the chopped peppers and coriander into the avocado mixture and season with salt and plenty of pepper. Just before serving, sprinkle a little extra coriander on top to garnish.

SERVES	PREP
6	15 mins

INGREDIENTS

juice of 2 lemons

3 tbsp extra virgin olive oil

3 ripe avocados

2 small red peppers

30g/1⅛oz fresh coriander, plus extra to garnish

salt and freshly ground black pepper

salsa verde
a salsa with a difference

TO MAKE THE SALSA VERDE

- Core, deseed and finely chop the chillies. Peel, deseed and dice the cucumber.
- Put the chopped chilli, coriander, parsley, mint, breadcrumbs, garlic, olive oil and lime juice in the food processor. Pulse until a coarse paste is formed. Add the salt and blitz again.
- Transfer the salsa to a serving bowl and fold in the diced cucumber. Taste and season with a little more salt if required.

SERVES	PREP
6	10 mins

INGREDIENTS

1–2 green chillies, according to taste

1 large cucumber

100g/3½oz fresh coriander

30g/1oz fresh flat-leaf parsley

15g/½oz fresh mint leaves

35g/1¼oz fresh white or brown breadcrumbs

1 garlic clove

120ml/3¾fl oz extra virgin olive oil

juice of 2 limes

1 tsp sea salt

fresh tomato salsa
it's the zingy lime that works so well

TO MAKE THE TOMATO SALSA

- Slice and then finely dice the tomatoes. Finely chop the coriander and parsley. Core, deseed and very finely chop the chilli, if using.
- Put the lime juice in a bowl. Add the sugar and stir until dissolved. Add the olive oil, tomatoes, chilli, coriander and parsley, and mix well together. Season to taste with salt and pepper. Transfer to a serving bowl to serve.

MAKES	PREP
6	10 mins

INGREDIENTS

8–10 ripe vine tomatoes

30g/1oz fresh coriander

30g/1oz fresh flat-leaf parsley

1 red chilli (optional)

juice of 2 limes

2 tbsp soft brown sugar

4 tbsp extra virgin olive oil

salt and freshly ground black pepper

spicy chicken

serve in a soft tortilla wrap and a napkin, tied together with string

SERVES	PREP & COOKING
6	25 mins (plus marinating time)

TO MAKE THE SPICY CHICKEN

♥ To make the marinade, put all the ingredients in a large bowl and stir well together until the sugar has dissolved.

♥ Cut the chicken into bite-sized chunks. Add to the marinade and mix together with your hands to make sure that the meat is well coated in the marinade. Leave at room temperature to marinate for 1 hour.

♥ Thinly slice the onions. Heat the oil in a large non-stick saucepan, add the onions and fry for about 5 minutes, until softened and slightly crispy. Add the mixed spice and garlic and cook for about 10 seconds, stirring all the time until the aroma is released.

♥ Add the chicken to the pan and cook, over a high heat, for 3 minutes. Add the tomato purée, brown sugar, cinnamon, cocoa powder, chilli flakes (if you're having it extra spicy!) and salt to the pan and then pour in the water. Stir, bring to the boil and then reduce the heat to low. Cover and allow to simmer for 10 minutes until the sauce has reduced and thickened slightly. Season to taste with pepper.

♥ Sprinkle over the coriander to garnish and serve with tortilla wraps or tacos, plenty of shredded crispy lettuce, grated cheese, jalapeño soured cream sauce, guacamole, salsa verde and fresh tomato salsa.

INGREDIENTS

6 skinless chicken breasts, organic/free-range

2 red onions

2 tbsp olive oil

1 tsp mixed spice

2 garlic cloves, crushed

200g/7oz tomato purée

3 tbsp brown sugar

2 tsp ground cinnamon

1 tbsp cocoa powder

1– 1½ tsp dried chilli flakes, to taste (optional)

1 tsp salt

300ml/10fl oz water

freshly ground black pepper

1 tbsp chopped fresh coriander, to garnish

FOR THE MARINADE

juice of 1 lime

2 tsp sugar

1 tsp dried oregano

2 red chillies, deseeded and finely chopped

TO SERVE

12 tortilla wraps or tacos

shredded crisp lettuce

grated Cheddar cheese

jalapeño soured cream sauce

guacamole

salsa verde

fresh tomato salsa

Fiesta

♥ halloween ♥

*For me, it's less about the trick,
and more about the treat!*

Gothic drama
*A fabulous key with a gravestone tag
sets the scene – inviting your guests to
'come and share the scare'. If they dare!*

I find Halloween irresistible… it's the perfect opportunity for children and grown-ups to get together, dress up, feast and party! Falling at the start of the winter season, when the evenings are darker and the nights are chillier, Halloween can be fun in as scary a way as you want it to be. The key is to know your audience – I remember my children loving the whole witches on broomsticks and 'woo-hooing' ghosts thing when they were younger, whereas for teenagers it's all about blood and gore and vampires. And adults – well, they love a bit of the theatrical! For inspiration, think of your favourite spooky movie, and be as elaborate as you like recreating the scary atmosphere – cobwebs, spiders, masses of candles, dark drapes. A few hidden bowls of dry ice will create an unnervingly effective smoky backdrop, and placed below a window are great for enticing brave trick or treaters to knock at the door! And don't forget a creepy soundtrack – ghosts wailing, creaking doors opening or a selection of thrilling monster tracks are sure to add to the party atmosphere! A splash of horror with a dose of drama and humour make for a wonderful party theme. For food and decor, go for a colour scheme inspired by those rich autumnal oranges of pumpkins and gourds, which work so brilliantly against black. So let your imagination go wild and enjoy creating your very own creepy wonderland with masses of fun and treats!

Blaze of glory
In America, neighbours have great fun trying to outdo each other with incredible Halloween displays outside their houses.

pesto tart

serve on a wooden board for a relaxed, rustic look

TO MAKE THE TART

- ♥ If you are really short for time, you can buy a good quality pre-prepared pesto sauce from the deli section in supermarkets but, at all costs, avoid the versions available in jars as they are too acidic and far removed from the true flavour of pesto. You will need 190g/6½oz.
- ♥ To make the pesto sauce, put the pine kernels in a large frying pan and, shaking the pan all the time so that they do not burn, dry-fry over a high heat until golden brown. Remove from the heat and leave to cool.
- ♥ Put the toasted pine kernels, basil and garlic into a blender and blitz until smooth. On a low speed, gradually drizzle in the oil until combined. Alternatively, put the toasted pine kernels, basil and garlic in a mortar and pound with a pestle until smooth. Add 2 tablespoons of the oil at a time and grind until incorporated.
- ♥ Stir the Parmesan cheese into the mixture until it forms a smooth paste.
- ♥ To make the tart, preheat the oven to 200°C/400°F/Gas 6. Line a large baking sheet with baking paper.
- ♥ Place the puff pastry on the prepared baking sheet and roll out to a rectangle measuring about 35x25cm/14x10in.
- ♥ Put the ricotta cheese and nutmeg in a bowl and mix together.
- ♥ Spread the pesto all over the puff pastry, leaving a 2.5cm/1in border around the edge. Using a teaspoon, put dollops of the ricotta all over the pesto and sprinkle the ricotta with the Parmesan cheese. Brush the pastry edge with the beaten egg to glaze.
- ♥ Bake in the oven for 20 minutes, until golden. Serve scattered with torn basil leaves to garnish, if wished.

SERVES
6

PREP/COOKING
15–30 mins/20 mins

INGREDIENTS

500g/1lb 2oz puff pastry

200g/7oz ricotta cheese

½ tsp grated nutmeg

3 tbsp freshly grated Parmesan cheese

1 small egg, beaten, to glaze

handful of fresh basil leaves, to garnish (optional)

FOR THE PESTO SAUCE

50g/1¾oz pine kernels

50g/1¾oz fresh basil leaves

3 garlic cloves

100ml/3½fl oz extra virgin olive oil

125g/4½oz freshly grated Parmesan cheese

Parents

pumpkin cupcakes
a treat for children of all ages

TO MAKE THE CUPCAKES

♥ Preheat the oven to 180°C/350°F/Gas 4. Line 2 8-hole muffin tins with paper cases.

♥ Put the butter, caster sugar and muscovado sugar in a large bowl and whisk together until light and fluffy. Add the eggs, 1 at a time, and whisk into the mixture. Stir in the pumpkin purée. Stir in the milk, replacing 1 tablespoon of the milk with brandy, if using.

♥ Sift the flour, baking powder, bicarbonate of soda, salt, ginger, cinnamon and nutmeg into another bowl. Stir in the raisins and/or stem ginger, if using.

♥ Add half the flour mixture to the pumpkin mixture and stir until combined. Add the remaining flour and stir until smooth. Spoon the mixture equally into the paper cases.

♥ Bake in the oven for 25–30 minutes, until golden and springy to the touch. Cool in the tin for 2–3 minutes before transferring to a wire rack to cool completely.

♥ To make the icing, put the cream cheese and butter in a large bowl and beat together until smooth. Sift in half the icing sugar, beat together and then sift in the remaining icing sugar and beat together until smooth. Put half the icing in another bowl and add a few drops of green food colouring to one bowl and orange to the other bowl, and stir until evenly coloured.

♥ When the cupcakes are cold, generously ice the tops with either the green or orange icing.

MAKES	PREP/COOKING
16	35 mins/25–30 mins

INGREDIENTS

115g/4oz butter, softened

130g/4¾oz golden caster sugar

130g/4¾oz light brown muscovado sugar

2 medium eggs

260g/9¼oz pumpkin purée

160ml/5½fl oz milk

1 tbsp brandy (optional)

280g/10oz plain white flour

3 tsp baking powder

½ tsp bicarbonate of soda

¼ tsp salt

½ tsp ground ginger

1 tsp ground cinnamon

¼ tsp grated nutmeg

60g/2¼oz raisins (optional)

50g/1¾oz stem ginger, chopped (optional)

FOR THE ICING

150g/5½oz full-fat soft cream cheese

50g/¾oz butter, at room temperature

325g/11½oz icing sugar

green and orange food colouring

endive salad

something a little more fresh and healthy

TO MAKE THE SALAD

- ♥ Separate the outer leaves from the heads of endive and slice the inner cores into wedges. Arrange on a serving platter or in a bowl.
- ♥ To make the dressing, stir the honey or maple syrup into the vinegar until blended together. Stir in the salt and the mustard until smooth. Season generously with pepper. Whisk in the olive oil until it has amalgamated.
- ♥ Pour the dressing over the prepared endive and sprinkle over the parsley.

SERVES   **PREP**
6   10 mins

INGREDIENTS
4 white endives
4 red endives
handful of finely chopped
    fresh flat-leaf parsley

FOR THE DRESSING
3 tsp clear honey or maple syrup
3 tbsp sherry vinegar
½ tsp salt
2 tsp Dijon mustard
5 tbsp extra virgin olive oil
freshly ground black pepper

Key to success (left)
You can sometimes find amazing old-fashioned keys at car boot sales. The older and more battered they are, the better.

Biscuit cutters (right)
Halloween-themed biscuit cutters are inexpensive to buy but have effective results.

Black out
A cluster of black candles in black hurricane lamps looks very dramatic.

Sweet treats
Halloween is traditionally overloaded with sugary treats, so also offer some savoury food options to balance out the sweet intake!

Accessorize
Vibrant pumpkin orange against black always looks dramatic, and gives you an excellent base for your colour scheme.

Pile up the table (right)
Pumpkins and gourdes interspersed with scary spiders will be sure to both spook and delight your guests!

Mini pumpkins (left)
Scooped up autumn leaves from your garden and mini pumpkins make a simple but gorgeous table feature.

Toffee apple delight
Sticky, gooey and a definite treat! And hey, at least the apple inside is healthy!